CUTTHROAT AND CAMPFIRE TALES

Cutthroat
& Campfire Tales

The Fly-Fishing Heritage of the West

John H. Monnett

Pruett Publishing Boulder, Colorado 1988

1 2 3 4 5 6 7 8 9

Design by Linda Seals, B. Vader Design/Production
Composition by Deborah M. Ingalls, War of Words Typography

LIBRARY OF CONGRESS CATALOGING-IN-PUBLICATION DATA

Monnett, John H.
    Cutthroat and campfire tales: the fly-fishing heritage of the
  West / by John H. Monnett.
        p.   cm.
    Bibliography: p.
    ISBN 0-87108-755-3 (paperback)
    ISBN 0-87108-782-0 (hardcover)
    1. Fly fishing–West (U.S.)   I. Title.
  SH456.M65 1988   88-23442
    799.1′2–dc19   CIP

Contents

This book is dedicated to Uncle Bill, who taught me many things, including how to cast a fly to a rising trout.

Prologue

Ever since the publication in Britain of Izaac Walton's *The Compleat Angler* in the seventeenth century, devotees of the gentle art of fly-fishing have sought to interpret the history of their timeless sport. I have often pondered in my imagination what the courtly Walton might have seen as he wandered the banks of Renaissance England's fabled chalk streams. Perhaps he noticed puffs of white clouds floating lazily on the summer breeze. Undoubtedly he smelled the fragrance of ripening grass on the pastoral hillsides in May. Maybe he even observed the dusky ruins of a twelfth-century castle beside an ancient millpond, or barn swallows darting across a pastel sky. Of course Walton remained constantly attuned to the subtle rise of the trout, and soon his long rod would arch radically above the crystalline waters, tight to a good fish.

Those of you who are versed in the tradition of fly-fishing will know that in actuality, the written record of "the gentle art" goes back two and a half centuries before the age of Walton. You will know that one of the earliest essays on the subject of sport-fishing was the *Treatise of Fishing with an Angle*, written in England sometime around 1496. You can trace the development of tandem wet fly-fishing through the nineteenth century. You sing the praises of Frederic Halford, who intrigued the world with the new concept of floating flies when he first published *Dry-Fly Fishing in Theory and Practice* in 1896. From the early twentieth century you hail the genius of the Englishman G.E.M. Skues and the skill of the American E.R. Hewitt for their advancements in the difficult art of nymphing. You may envision a tubercular, mustachioed little man named Theodore Gordon prowling the banks of the Neversink River in New York's Catskill Mountains at the turn of the twentieth century. The development of his impressionistic Quill Gordon dry fly and his erudite but lively articles written for the venerable sportsman's journal *Forest and Stream* have instructed and pleased generations of men and women enchanted with the sport of fly-fishing.

Although Gordon was not the first American to fish with floating flies, he certainly popularized the technique in his writing and has thus become identified with the dry fly in America. No one can deny that Gordon deserves high acclaim, symbolically at least, among fly-fishers in this country. His time-honored Catskill rivers, though dammed into oblivion in many regions, are still "Gordon Country," and they continue to be revered by many anglers throughout the country.

Through the efforts of the Theodore Gordon Flyfishers, many of the old Gordon haunts in the Catskills have been recently identified. In Manchester, Vermont, the American Museum of Fly Fishing has collected antique fishing tackle and numerous artifacts that illustrate the evolution of fly-fishing in the United States. Across the nation there is a rapidly growing interest in fly-fishing's early history and tradition. Most of this recent knowledge, however, only pertains to fishing on British and eastern waters.

Astonishingly, the American West shares little in the tradition. In a land where pristine wilderness trout streams still exist, where remarkable stories are told by our pioneer ancestors of huge trout in phenomenal numbers, there is little recorded in the great body of fishing literature that chronicles the remarkable pageant of western angling during the nineteenth and early twentieth centuries. In fact, the West has contributed much to the development of the sport. Our big, bushy fastwater flies (some of which would scare eastern purists), our long, strong, full-backboned rods and weighted nymphing techniques are special and deserve a place in the historical record. Moreover, the alluring stories of our ancestors, who recalled seemingly limitless numbers of trout from the eastern slopes of the Rockies to the far Cascade Mountains, likewise deserve recognition in the annals of fly-fishing. To this end I have endeavored to relate a few of the stories and traditions of western angling long ago.

When the first pioneers rumbled past the unbroken plains in their Conestoga wagons, the vast cordillera of the Rocky Mountains which met them literally teemed with native cutthroat trout. Farther west, in the High Sierras, the elusive golden trout thrived in cold, high-altitude streams. The lustrous grayling abounded in Montana and regions to the north. The colorful rainbow of the Pacific Coast, some of which made the annual journey to the sea along with prolific numbers of salmon, rounded out the astonishing abundance. An early sportsman in Colorado Territory of the 1860s by the name of J.W. Kelly reflected on what he perceived to be a limitless resource after a day of angling on the virgin headwaters of the Grand (Colorado) River, in what is today Rocky Mountain National Park. "In Grand [River]," Kelly noted in his fishing log, "the water is alive with trout. The summer's evening is enlivened for the tourist by watching the trout leap and play in the waters along the shores. Some of these trout pass the bounds of common belief, so large are they. One of them fills a platter nicely and makes a hearty meal for three or four people. They reach over ten pounds in size by [the] hundreds, and the smaller trout are despised by the natives, who throw them back, keeping only the larger ones for the table."

Kelly's description, unfortunately, reveals the attitude of consumption exhibited by early settlers in the West. To them, the natural resources of the frontier seemed inexhaustible. They thought that not only fish, but big game as well, especially the enormous herds of American bison that reached into the millions, would abound in the land forever. Kelly expressed this attitude quite accurately in his fishing log. "Long after this generation of fishermen have un-jointed their rods forever," he wrote, "the trout will leap unscared by the approach of man. The region [upper Colorado River] is too wide and wild to be fished out for half a century to come."

Unfortunately, by the turn of the twentieth century, most of the native cutthroat were long gone from Colorado River headwaters; gone the way of the buffalo. Today, populations of stunted eastern brook trout hold in their runs. The one thing Kelly and his brethren never fully understood was that even in the wilderness a sizeable population of fish and game could not sustain a growing human population for very long when unchecked by effective regulation or voluntary conservation.

I hope that the tales in this book will help instill a sense of conservation in the reader. With the ever-increasing popularity of limited kill fishing, and perhaps a sense of history, we may one day again enjoy the thrills of western angling enjoyed by our ancestors.

Unlike numerous other books on angling tradition, this volume is *not* an analysis of famous fishing writers of the past or the techniques they advanced. Neither is the book a detailed academic history of the development of the sport's "tools of the trade." Much of the heritage of fly-fishing in the West during the nineteenth century is simply embodied in the fabulous fishing that was to be had in thousands of miles of virgin wilderness water and the pioneer's reaction to that seemingly unending resource. The fishing trips and wilderness experiences we all dream about were commonplace during the nineteenth century, and these tales make for fascinating fishing stories in and of themselves while adding the vital theme of conservation to the list of angling topics suitable for historical interpretation. Certainly, some of the horror stories of wanton exploitation of trout resources in the past may shock you. But the majority of the book consists of stories about real people with whom the modern angler can identify.

So much of fly-fishing pleasure is in the personal bond the individual forms with the environment and the tradition. A letter written to the editor of *Fly Fisherman* magazine in 1987 perhaps expresses it in the simplest terms: "Often when I release a feisty native cutthroat . . . , I pause to reflect on my surroundings and on what has gone before me: The land, the people; What was the place like a hundred years ago?; What has the fish 'seen?' Surely [other sportsmen] are sensitive to this notion."

For this reason, I have broken with traditional style by interweaving each chapter with my own reflections, experiences and, I'm afraid on occasion, philosophy of life and trout-fishing. Philosophy is important in building tradition, and of what use is a knowledge of angling history if it does not moderate our attitudes in some enjoyable way when we venture forth upon stream or lake in our own times? Here is but one fly-fisher's highly personal perspective on the impact of the past upon the present—less a narrative history and more a celebration of tradition. I invite you then, to consider a more genteel age when the trout were large and the anglers few. Perhaps you, too, will develop a sense for the West's great angling heritage.

Of course, no book like this could have been completed without the efforts of others. I wish to express my gratitude to the staffs of the historical societies of Colorado, Wyoming, Montana, and Yellowstone National Park for their vital assistance. The librarians at the Western History Department of the Denver Public Library, Boulder

Public Library, University of Colorado, and the National Archives were terrific, as usual.

Special thanks goes to the American Museum of Fly Fishing in Manchester, Vermont, for providing useful information. For putting up with my questions about her father Ernest, thanks goes to Helen Blumenschein of Taos, New Mexico. Gratitude is also extended to John Gierach and Paul Schullery for reading the manuscript and making valuable suggestions. Finally, thanks is in order, once again, to my lovely wife Linda, for reading and criticizing each chapter from the perspective of a nonangler–"I depend on you, babe!"

For a Century to Come

The sleepy Missouri town where I began my love affair with fly-fishing was lost in time. With the exception of red cobblestone streets, moderate automobile traffic, and modern street lighting, its appearance was much the same as it had been a century ago. An old courthouse was the absolute soul of the tiny community. For as long as anyone could remember, its venerable clock had chimed out the passing of people's lives from a Gothic watchtower of weathered native limestone, cloaked in runners of ancient ivy.

A short distance out of town, along a rutted country road flanked by ferns and thick stands of native oak, was a spring-fed trout stream, charming in its setting. It ran unrestricted through the bosom of a small valley for about two miles in an east to west direction. Beginning with the cold winds of March, anglers from the city would descend on the little stream. I would usually be among them. We would stand shivering in icy dawn waters, as thick clouds of white mist rose through the valley and settled along the crest of adjacent ridges, which were starting to come to life at that time of the year with a rich carpet of sumac and May apples.

On weekend mornings throughout the season, anglers might stand shoulder to shoulder, casting small streamers, Wooly Worms, or Royal Coachman wet flies upstream as best they could. When conditions were especially crowded, which was usually the norm, the gaudy flies might be cast toward the far bank of a long, slick pool or gentle riffle and then stripped back toward the angler with a slow, deliberate twitching motion. The abundantly stocked rainbows would always cooperate, and by late morning everyone would be strutting along the banks showing off fine stringers of trout. A nearby lodge and tackle shop, constructed of logs in the 1940s, became the center for conversation by noon. Along the walls of the old lodge were photographs of fishermen plying the waters of the little stream back in the '30s. Mounts of big trout hung over the counter where wooden display trays full of locally tied flies enticed customers. Over in a dusty corner was a large, upright freezer where anglers could store their trout in plastic bags, labeled with their name and address.

Those who caught big fish would place their trophies conspicuously toward the front of the freezer and write their names in large letters on the clear plastic bags. It was sort of the local game to play. Anyone who brought in a fish of three pounds or over would be awarded a "lunker pin" by the proprietor of the lodge to wear on his or her fishing vest. Several local anglers had as many as twenty pins glaring from their vests and hats, taunting the less fortunate. No one ever considered releasing fish. After all, the stream was managed on a strictly put-and-take basis with silvery rainbows stocked almost daily from a nearby hatchery.

Several years after I received my initial tutelage on the little stream, I moved out West. At that time I really made no distinction in my mind between hatchery-raised trout and stream-spawned wild fish. Whatever their origin, I had learned through years of subtle conditioning that a "real fisherman" killed fish.

In the Rockies I fished several streams to which I had made annual pilgrimages since childhood. Two of these streams were said to be "overpopulated with small brook trout." The bag limit allowed me to kill eight brookies under eight inches in addition to the regular limit. The killing of fish was even good conservation! The only thing was—these streams also contained many brown trout, some of them quite large. I killed the browns too. I would make a ritual of cleaning them with an antique knife, which I fantasized had been used to dress innumerable huge fish in frontier times. I was quite proud of my catches.

One day I caught a sixteen-inch brown in one of the small streams, my first sizeable fish on a nymph. I brought it home and showed it off with pride. The next week I returned to the same pool that had given me such pleasure battling that brown. This time I only caught eight-inch brookies. The next time too, eight-inch brookies—and the next, and the next. In fact, I never again caught a brown exceeding

nine inches from that spot—except once. One fine fall afternoon I hooked a twelve-inch brown. I started to unhook the #18 Humpy from the lip of the firm-bodied, hook-jawed male and place the fish in my creel when I remembered the sixteen-incher from two years before. For no apparent reason, I actually felt something like *sympathy* for this trout. I reasoned that if I killed it, it would be . . . *gone*. Perhaps I would never catch another brown from this spot. But if I released the fish, I would at least know that a nice brown *would be there*, whether or not I ever caught it again. Gently, I revived the brown and watched it slowly swim away.

From that time forward I started releasing more and more trout. But it didn't happen all at once. In fact, when I first started reading the arguments in favor of limiting the kill, which were just starting to appear in the sporting journals at that time, I actually found them to be very elitist. It took time to acquire the habit. In fact, I actually had to fish waters restricted by law to catch and release so I would be forced to resist temptation. Today, I still might kill a couple of fish for a camp supper. The tradition of killing fish in the West is a strong one.

Shortly after the founding of any new community on the far western frontier, fishing became a common recreational pursuit in a land devoid of most organized recreational pursuits. The attractions of nature and a few log and tar paper saloons were about the only amusement people had during the early years of their communities. In addition, fur trappers, explorers, and miners who were thrust abruptly into virgin wilderness actually depended to a greater or lesser degree upon trout populations for food.

On these raw, new frontiers of the West, devoid in the early years of formal laws governing natural resources, fish were taken in abundance by rod and reel, even overharvested from the beginning, for the purposes of food and sport—in some cases the two were viewed as synonymous. Everyone believed that the natural resources of the West would last forever. Unlike the East, there were hundreds of thousands of miles of wilderness, and very few people. Just as the open range cattle ranchers could never comprehend the decimation of rangelands from Canada to Texas, neither could market fishermen and sportsmen envision the end of trout resources in individual territories, each one the size of New England.

But within a very short time, trout vanished from streams near sparsely populated frontier communities. It was not the killing of hundreds of trout each week by true sportsmen that did most of this damage, however. Mining and logging practices took a far greater toll, as did, ironically, attempts by local governments on the frontier to improve sport-fishing through the introduction of exotic fish species. Add to this the harvesting of trout for market by dynamiting lakes and streams, and you have greater damage done to native trout populations than that inflicted by all the "trout hogs" in the West combined.

Nevertheless, the ethic of one's *right* to harvest an abundance of fish by rod and reel on public land became well ingrained in the western psyche from the beginning—a part of the democratic pioneer spirit. The nineteenth-century concept of "sportsmanship" simply did not include releasing fish. Such a practice was considered bizarre. "Free meat" was the goal; fooling the fish was merely the "sporting" means to that end. Such was the code of the frontier. Consequently, opposition to proposals for regulating trout resources (or anything else for that matter) came to characterize western logic, and that logic has persisted, in some form, right down to the present day—it's part of our heritage, like the right to bear firearms.

Among the first American sport-fishers in the West to record their adventures were members of the Lewis and Clark Expedition. It is unknown whether any members of the expedition fished with flies during the landmark trip, but on June 13, 1805, while camped on the upper Missouri River, Lewis wrote in his journal regarding the physical appearance of some strange, freshly caught trout, which measured "from 16–23 inches in length." Distinguishing them from the familiar eastern brook trout, Lewis wrote:

> "These are furnished with long teeth on the pallet and tongue and have generally a small dash of red on each side behind the front ventral fins; the flesh is of a pale yellowish red, or when in good order, of a rose red."

Certainly Lewis and Clark paved the way through much of the West's prime trout, steelhead, and salmon country for future explorers and settlers. Unfortunately, the new species of trout they officially discovered and described, *Salmo clarki*, only much later referred to as "cutthroat," would, within about seventy years or so, become devastated by overharvest and indiscriminate mining and logging practices.

The early fur trappers who came west on the heels of Lewis and Clark utilized trout for food, learning from mountain dwelling Indians how to spear them with regularity. There are few records to inform us whether or not any of the mountain men were fly-fishers, but some of them boasted of catching large trout on rod and reel in the deep, cool waters of Yellowstone Lake, and then cooking the fish in the upper, hot waters of the lake as the creatures were pulled out of the water. They never even had to take the fish off the hook. These stories sound like tall tales until you consider that for years, tourists would dunk live fish on the line into the famous fishing cone, a hot thermal spring along the shore of the lake. The practice was not outlawed until the twentieth century. In December 1911, an article in *Forest and Stream* reported that:

> owing to complaints received by the Department of the Interior from the American Humane Association regarding the cruelty of this method of cooking fish, the tourist will be compelled to carry a club with him and kill his fish by beating it on the head or by stabbing it with his knife. The superintendent of the park has been instructed to incorporate such a regulation in the draft of the park rules to be issued for the season of 1912.

During the era of the fur trade, the numbers of beaver men setting their traps in the mountain West were hardly large enough to do irreparable damage to trout populations. But such was not the case during the mining and ranching eras that followed. Beginning in the 1850s and continuing for forty years or so, scores of mining towns sprang up in California, Nevada, Colorado, and finally the northern Rockies and the Southwest. Tailings and other mining wastes did most of the damage, but the attitudes of some sport-fishers of the day didn't help either.

The early diaries of fishermen at this time evidenced a belief that huge trout populations would last for at least a century to come. Scientific understanding regarding the fragile nature of native fisheries was either disregarded when anglers considered the expansiveness of the West, or it simply did not reach many people living in the region. During the initial years of any new mining camp, market fishermen took a heavy toll on trout populations. In 1871 a group of local boys literally kept Georgetown and Central City, Colorado, supplied with fresh trout from nearby streams. The use of dynamite made market fishing a profitable business. But sport-fishers were active too. The damage they inflicted was considerably less than that of the mining operations, but the fact that they claimed to be sportsmen makes their activity only the more horrifying to modern anglers.

As capital was accumulated by lucky individuals, and as crude frontier towns grew into thriving metropolises, affluent residents of the West would vacation in the nearby mountains, where they experienced fishing success that would astound fly-fishers of the twentieth century. With the coming of the railroads, remote waters could be reached quite rapidly, and the railroad companies advertised in their literature the fabulous fishing to be had along their routes. Eventually, the railroad companies even lured eastern sportsmen to the famed waters and game ranges of the "Wild West." The popular belief today is that "true" sportsmen recognized before it was too late that both fish and game resources in the West were being decimated. They supposedly banded together to form fishing and hunting clubs for the purpose of managing resources and to lobby for bag limits and other regulations. In the East there are some striking examples of this as early as the 1860s, even though many brook trout populations were already decimated by the time these sportsmen took action.

This early conservation movement came late to the West—not until the 1880s. To some extent this was simply a result of western frontiers being settled later than anywhere else. But even at the turn of the century, the anti-conservation forces in the region were more vocal than were the concerned sportsmen. Boosters, trying to lure both new residents and tourists alike, painted the picture that western trout resources were unlimited, and local media supported the illusion. As late as 1912, an article in *Field and Farm Magazine*, designed to lure eastern tourists to Wyoming's Big Laramie River, boasted:

> I have seen a nine-pound German brown trout taken from the river and some rainbow even larger. The law allows a daily catch of twenty pounds, but I have never noticed anyone weighing his basket, and have known of individuals catching more than one hundred in a day.

In addition, the rural, egalitarian nature of the West did not produce as many elite sportsmen's clubs concerned with conservation as did the numerous urban centers of the East. Although California had an organization on the McCloud River by 1878, and San Francisco had at least two clubs a few years later, the movement did not proliferate in most of the rural West before the twentieth century. So there they were, with thousands of acres of public domain surrounding them, in a land where, they felt, the trout could never be wiped out, a land where writers in the regional sporting journals actually boasted of violating bag limits as if it were socially acceptable practice. In the East, to some degree, a "true" sportsman, possessing enlightened conservationist attitudes, could frequently be identified by his pedigree. In the West, however, it was not always that easy to differentiate an angler who fished purely for sport from a person trying to provide necessary food, or for that matter, from a plain old "game hog." The term "sportsman" simply can't be defined very well in the West before the end of the nineteenth century.

By the late 1870s and early 1880s, about the same time that hunters from both the East and the West helped decimate the buffalo by shooting the animals from the windows of railroad cars, the railroads were unloading sportsmen to fish waters throughout the West. Already damaged, many trout populations were given the coup de grace. Examples abound. In 1873 the *Rocky Mountain News* reported that "Messrs. Rice and Hatfield, noted Denver sportsmen, returned from a fishing vacation in South Park [Colorado]." The two men caught over "850 pounds, and shipped them to Denver." They then proceeded to Poncha Pass where they caught an additional 650 pounds. The men only fished for five days. In August 1874, a group of five railroad executives traveled to the headwaters of the Cache la Poudre River in Colorado Territory for a week's sport-fishing. In four days' time the party, using flies, caught over 1000 trout, "many of them weighing over two pounds each." In 1876 the *Fort Collins Express* reported that over five tons of trout were taken in the Poudre River during the summer months alone. The article also made clear that market fishermen were not active on the Poudre that summer.

One of the most horrifying tales involved a party of five wealthy Denver sportsmen, including David Moffat and Walter Cheesman, two of the city's business elite and civic leaders. The *Rocky Mountain News* enthusiastically reported on their success using Coachman and Grey Hackle wet flies in 1876:

> They struck out for the upper Cache la Poudre. Here they spent several days fishing for trout. There was no limit to the sport. Altogether about a thousand trout were landed, varying from a half to two and a half pounds in weight. They packed up 100 pounds of the largest and choicest ones and started home with them, but upon reaching the railroad and opening the boxes it was found that the fish had spoiled on their hands, and they were all thrown away.

In less accessible waters as well, the exploitation went on. In 1877 the *News* ran a story about a man named Peck who lived along the banks of the upper Rio Grande River. Peck ran a hotel and caught trout to feed his guests. "Landlord Peck is a famous fisherman," noted the *News*. "With rod and fly he has this year caught and served on his

own table over thirty-four hundred pounds of trout. Most of them have been taken within a half mile of his door."

By the 1870s the fabulous hunting and fishing to be had in the West not only attracted wealthy sportsmen from the East but the noble gentry of Europe as well. Lord Gore employed the old mountain man Jim Bridger to guide him on extended trips through the Rockies, where he slaughtered big game and fish with reckless abandon. In 1874 none other than William "Buffalo Bill" Cody and the flamboyant George Armstrong Custer guided the young Grand Duke Alexis of Russia on a "Grand Buffalo Hunt" across the Nebraska prairie. The railroad transported the royal entourage, which boasted champagne and caviar served on sterling silver dinnerware to complement the fare of buffalo and antelope steaks served during the gala evening parties.

In numerous cases many wealthy Europeans, especially those of British or Scottish extraction, became so enthralled with the perceived romance of the American West that they took up residence as part-time ranchers. One such Englishman was the fourth Earl of Dunraven, who by 1876 was trying to buy up the whole of Estes Park, Colorado, as a private game and fish preserve for his own use. As was customary throughout the ranching frontier of the West, the Earl required all of his cowboys to file for their 160 acres under the Homestead Act, lay down a few logs to represent a cabin, and then sell their "proved-up" claims to Dunraven. The Earl finally tired of his estate (when most of the game and fish were gone) in the 1880s and sold out, but for a time he monopolized much of the beautiful land that today flanks the eastern borders of Rocky Mountain National Park.

Naturally, these wealthy landowners (individuals, not clubs concerned about the diminishing game and fish) kept their land and its resources to be used exclusively by themselves and their guests. Unfortunately, this practice did not always contribute to the conservation of game and fish as it did in the East where the wealthy sporting clubs often purchased large tracts of land and managed them properly. During an outing on Dunraven's estate in August 1885, for example, a small party of three guests killed between 2500 and 3000 trout in ten days.

This attitude of consumption did not always go unchallenged. Appalled by the presence of men like Dunraven, not to mention the abuses of market fishing, a few foresighted people began calling for legal controls by the mid-1870s. Colorado was the first territory in the Rocky Mountain West to attain statehood. With the admission to the union of the Centennial State, concerned Coloradoans began lobbying their first state legislature for effective bag limits. A reporter for the *Rocky Mountain News* stated in 1876 that:

The entire northern portion of Colorado needs some efficient means of protection for both fish and game, since both are rapidly disappearing. . . . It will be a serious blow to Colorado when the news goes forth that our hunting and fishing is no longer first class, and any measure of relief that can be reached should be adopted. It is of the utmost importance that something should be done to render the present [territorial] law operative, or to enact one that will "stick."

Under territorial law, which gave wide administrative discretion to the federal government in Washington, bag limits simply were not enforced on the frontier with much regularity by local officials. In fact, public resources actually were viewed by many as a national "crop" to be harvested by enterprising individuals. In 1877 Colorado empowered a state fish commissioner to deal with the problems. In 1897 a formal Department of Forestry, Game and Fish was established by the legislature. Other western territories followed suit upon their admission to statehood. It wasn't until the twentieth century, however, that game laws would "stick." In truth, distances and relatively sparse populations made law enforcement almost impossible. In many cases people flaunted their open violation of the laws, and booster literature began at this time to boast that in Colorado, "bag limits on fish are not actively enforced."

The attitudes of the anti-conservationists were well voiced by the *News* at the time of statehood: "In some portions of the state the abundance of fish render such legislation [bag limits] not only unnecessary but oppressive." This belief, which tolerated land and resource monopolizers like the Earl of Dunraven, mirrored a basic double standard inherent in many westerners of the late nineteenth century. From their experience with the inadequacy of the territorial system, many citizens abhorred regulation in any form, believing it their pioneer right to partake freely and equally of nature's abundance. But when these same citizens attained any measure of wealth and power themselves, they locked up large blocks of land (and water) and restricted its use for their own exploitation. In either case, nature came out the loser. The attitude of a largely laissez faire federal government before 1901 aided the anti-conservationist cause by stressing the consumption of natural resources to speed industrialization and "progress" throughout the rapidly urbanizing nation. If effective laws were to stick, and just as importantly, if a realistic ethic governing sportsmanship was to be created, it would have to come at a higher level, a nongovernmental higher level, which could appeal to sportsmen's sensibilities at the grass roots.

Fortunately, the forerunners of the "muckrakers" were starting to catch the attention in the popular media of many literate Americans during the last three decades of the nineteenth century. Not only did U.S. Steel and Standard Oil come under attack by the turn of the century, but indiscriminate exploitation of fish and game resources were exposed as well. One of the first journals for sportsmen was *Forest and Stream*, founded in 1873 by Charles Hallock. Even during its earliest years editorials appealed for conservation. Given the racial climate of the times, however, the most inflammatory articles of the '70s weren't necessarily leveled against Anglo-Americans. Consider an editorial by a concerned reader who spoke out against the presence of Washoe Indians, "camped all summer long" along the shores of Lake Tahoe, spearing trout for sale in Carson City and Virginia City. "500 pounds per day for a single Indian." The article went on to describe how many of the fish were not even sent to market, being used instead to pay off debts at the poker tables.

In 1896, John R. Burkhard founded *Western Field & Stream Magazine*. The next year the magazine was being published in New York, the name *Western* was dropped from the title, and a publishing legend was born. Eltrige Warner took over the publication in 1907 and proceeded to turn *Field & Stream* into one of the nation's most beloved sporting magazines. Warner himself was an outspoken conservationist who helped secure much important legislation, including the federal Migratory Bird Act. By 1930 *Field & Stream* and *Forest and Stream* had merged. There were other important journals as well. The *American Sportsman* (1871), *American Field* (1874), and the *American Angler* (1881) all attempted to instill the British tradition of game and fish management in the American mind. Unquestionably, these publications helped to shape public opinion toward regulation during the waning years of the nineteenth century and the early years of the twentieth.

Perhaps the greatest name of the day associated with the budding conservation movement in the U.S. was George Bird Grinnell, the crusading editor of *Forest and Stream* between 1880 and 1911. From 1876 to 1880, he had been the natural history editor of the publication. During these years, Grinnell turned *Forest and Stream* into the premier voice for change in attitudes toward game and fish management, and conservation of natural resources in general. An ethnologist on the staff of Yale's Peabody Museum, Grinnell made annual trips to the West. There he got to know the Cheyenne and Pawnee as his brothers. He served as naturalist on General George Armstrong Custer's expedition to the Black Hills in 1874. He toured Yellowstone National Park in 1875, saw the decimation of the buffalo, and even participated in E.H. Harriman's Alaska expedition in 1899. He started the movement that became the National Audubon Society. He was a valued advisor to President Theodore Roosevelt and authored treatises that eventually resulted in the creation of Glacier National Park. He was often referred to as "the father of American conservation."

During his years at *Forest and Stream*, Grinnell urged the passage of effective game laws for all states and territories. He published articles calling for the enforcement of laws and stiff penalties for violators. He helped pioneer efforts at fish culture and the preservation of forest lands and fish and wildlife habitat. Probably no other individual did as much to reshape attitudes of Americans toward fish and wildlife regulation. Grinnell was himself a sportsman, and by the 1880s he had given definition to the term. Indeed, historian John F. Reiger, writing in *American Sportsmen and the Origins of Conservation*, argues that "American sportsmen were by far the single most important group in the making of conservation" in the U.S.

By the 1880s, concerned sportsmen-conservationists, both East and West, were taking steps to replenish diminishing trout resources. If the state failed, communities, private sporting clubs, if they existed, and individuals took up the cause locally. In the West both state wildlife agencies and private citizens opened trout hatcheries for the propagation of fish to replenish depleted streams and lakes. Unfortunately, this well-meaning enterprise spelled doom for many remaining cutthroat trout, "Lewis's fish," which dominated the West before the coming of the white man. Where spring-spawning rainbows were introduced, the cutthroat was "bred out." Neither could the cutthroats compete with prolific brook trout in waters where the eastern species was introduced, nor could they compete with brown trout from Europe which first arrived in the U.S. in the early 1880s and eventually found their way west on the railroads. Nevertheless, these early stocking efforts paid off to some extent by furnishing fish to remote waters that were historically barren or overharvested. By the late 1890s, catches of giant rainbows, "many exceeding 10 pounds" were being reported for large rivers like Colorado's Gunnison.

Unfortunately, the new conservation ethic, which stressed the passage of bag limits, did not yet advocate a catch-and-release philosophy. Even back East creeling trout was still the well-accepted norm among many anglers at the turn of the century. A 1912 editorial appearing in *Forest and Stream* enthusiastically reported that over 3800 trout were creeled on one opening day in the late 1890s along a short stretch of a Catskill river. "One boy caught three strings and sold them for five dollars apiece," the reporter admiringly stated. That reporter was none other than Theodore Gordon. An article advising new anglers in the art of fly-fishing and appearing in the *Denver Post*

in April 1929 advised the neophyte fly-fisher that if a fish "be of legal size it is customary to kill it by whacking it on the head with the butt of a knife or nearby stone."

By the third decade of the twentieth century at the latest, most true sport-fishers in the West realized full well the necessity of bag limits and vigorous enforcement of the laws. Private organizations like the Wigwam Club along the South Platte River might preempt rich stretches of water, but such groups in the West joined their eastern counterparts by 1930 in advocating the cause of conservation. With the founding of true grass-roots conservationist organizations beginning in the 1960s, national groups like Trout Unlimited and The Federation of Fly Fishers have made great inroads in establishing a limited kill philosophy among dedicated fly-fishers throughout the nation.

Perhaps more importantly, their efforts at stream habitat improvement, opposition to dam building, which hampered conservation efforts beginning with the Great Depression and the New Deal of the '30s, and their dedication to the goals of environmental education in general, may one day enable the fly-fisher of the twenty-first century to at least sample trout numbers as they existed during the time of our ancestors.

Such a goal can be accomplished, however, only with restricted kill limits in certain waters where such regulations indeed will increase both the size and the numbers of trout. Times change, and so too must the definition of sportsmanship. Heritage and tradition, like the U.S. Constitution, are not strictly constructed concepts. In the end, the real choice is up to each of us as individuals.

In Search of Western Natives

I enjoy spending August evenings fishing the Madison River. The scenery along the thirty-mile drive from West Yellowstone, by itself, is worth the trip. U.S. Highway 287 snakes its way along the north shore of Hebgen Lake where scores of husky rainbows sip tiny black-and-white tricos from the surface waters on still summer mornings. Past Quake Lake in Madison Canyon the road finally emerges into a beautiful valley with sweeping mountain vistas. The little valley is curiously named Missouri Flats. After viewing this region for the first time I fully understood why Montana is called Big Sky Country. I turn off next to a bridge that crosses the river along a road heading south, toward Reynolds Pass and Henry's Lake down in Idaho. There is a parking spot here on a state controlled fishing access area. The entrance to the parking spot is choked with rocks and is quite bumpy. During the morning hours, some of the guides from West Yellowstone launch their McKenzie River drift boats at this point to fish the famed catch-and-release section of the upper river.

After uncasing my fly rod and rolling on a pair of neoprene waders, I begin a short hike downstream. To the north, the Madison Range in the Beaverhead National Forest rises above me, pointing toward an endless sky. I immediately recognize 11,286-foot Koch Peak. Very soon it will be bathed in the soothing alpenglow of a Rocky Mountain sunset. If an afternoon shower has blessed the valley, the pleasant fragrance of sage adds to the ambiance of the trek. The footing is surprisingly rough, however. Wet grass is slippery under my boots, and it's almost mandatory that I stumble in at least three gopher holes.

Of course the jaunt is worth the effort, because I am here to catch large trout, rainbows and browns. At times, the evening caddis hatches along this stretch of river can be incredible. Swarming clouds of the insects are thick, and I know that I will be obliged to switch on wipers for the drive home just to keep from being mesmerized by the little boogers as they light on my windshield. The larger fish generally hold at the edge of the swift, frothing channel where it's almost impossible to mend line quickly enough to keep a dry fly floating drag-free for the entire length of the drift. I spot a couple of three-pounders in this current, rolling up to capture emerging pupae, with only their backs and dorsal fins clearing the water. The fish can be quite selective. A small emerger pattern fished just under the surface is usually the right choice, however, and more often than not, the strike comes as the fly arcs below me at the end of the drift. Toward dusk the trout begin to rise more freely in the quieter water close to the bank. I switch to a small Elk Hair Caddis as the daylight rapidly fades around me. I am usually able to release two or three good fish on these evenings, maybe breaking off a couple more.

Twilight comes late to southwestern Montana, but eventually a pair of evening swallows begins to strafe the river in search of insects as the last amber glow from the sun pales on the horizon, and I begin my short walk to the rocky parking area. Back at the camper I usually strike up a lantern-light conversation with other anglers while munching a cold sandwich and gulping down an equally chilled cup of coffee from my ancient thermos. "Broke off a twenty-incher right at dusk," exclaims a Californian. "Yeah, I missed a wallhanger only about a hundred yards from here," boasts a professional-looking, Orvis-attired gentleman with Pennsylvania license plates. Inevitably someone asks, "Where ya all from?" and everybody is mildly surprised at the diverse geographical representation of fly-fishers congregated at the access area. During recent years, I actually have acquired the habit of counting license plates in this tiny parking space. To date I have tabulated licenses from exactly thirty-one states, including Alaska and Hawaii. California, Colorado, Michigan, Illinois, and New York seem to predominate (in that order).

On the trip back to West Yellowstone, I am amazed at how much attention is given these Montana waters. People literally drive thousands of miles every summer for a chance to match wits with large trout. Thank heavens for the no-kill regulations! Eventually my thoughts turn to the species of fish they have traveled so far to catch.

Californians drive from the West Coast to catch rainbows, a fish native to the Pacific Slope. New Englanders are well represented even though many bragging-sized browns still prowl certain eastern waters. And the throngs of anglers after cutthroats over on the Yellowstone River, inside the park, can be profuse. But most of these tourists fish the Yellowstone for the same reason people fish the Madison—lots of big trout. The particular species is usually only incidental to numbers and size, especially size.

I am just as glad as the next person that exotic species have been nurtured in waters historically devoid of fish or stripped of their native cutthroats by early market fishing. I am equally glad that many of these exotics here in the West are big, and I am just as eager as any easterner to travel here to catch the hard-fighting rainbows and browns for which the Madison River is world famous. But there is something deep in my psyche that irrevocably turns my thoughts to wild cutthroats in remote waters. Most of these colorful fish are not large, although some real "hogs" do exist in a few wilderness lakes. I guess it's just that they are, well, "natives" to my Rocky Mountain homeland. As a matter of fact, they are the only trout native to most of the Rocky Mountains. They were the fish known by the pioneers, and that is why, as I finally glimpse the approaching lights of West Yellowstone's Best Western Motel, I once again yearn to seek them out in the wild and remote places that constitute their remaining habitat.

Originally the range of the cutthroat trout extended over much of the western United States. With the purchase of the Louisiana Territory in 1803 and the eventual opening of the fur trade, American explorers and mountain men literally penetrated every nook and cranny of the mountainous West. They followed the river courses upstream in search of beaver. The hides were shipped East every year, where they would be fashioned into stylish hats to be worn in both Europe and America. To meet the growing demand for furs after 1820, the mountain men kept moving farther upriver in search of new trapping grounds. When a major river system became trapped out, they wandered up the tributary creeks and streams in their relentless search for profit. There were no towns or cities to meet the supply needs of these trappers, and for most of the year they had to live off the land until the spring rendezvous. It was natural that these wilderness wanderers would subsist, to a large extent, upon the fish populations located in the streams where they trapped. It was the mountain men who first extensively utilized the cutthroat trout. In years when big game became scarce, they may have depended heavily on this creature to sustain life.

From Prince William Sound in Alaska, south to the coastal regions of northern California, and inland to the mountain ranges of today's Southwest, the cutthroat thrived in abundance during the era of the fur trade. Throughout most of the Rocky Mountains there were no other competing trout. Cutthroats were kings in their historic watersheds. In times of geologic upheaval, long before the coming of the white man, *Salmo clarki* made its way into headwater creeks on both sides of the continental divide as the great glaciers that helped carve the Rocky Mountains receded toward towering summits. Approximately sixteen subspecies of cutthroats eventually evolved in western waters before man arrived on the scene. Prehistoric Indians became adept at spearing them for food. With the opening of the Oregon Trail during the 1830s, emigrants in one of the great mass migrations in history welcomed the chance to procure fresh meat when the wagon trains crossed mountain passes. The cutthroat provided them sustenance.

In certain regions some members of the species grew to enormous size. In fact, the largest nonanadromous western salmonids known to the pioneers were the huge Lahontan cutthroat trout of Pyramid Lake. Isolated in the Great Basin in what is today the state of Nevada, Pyramid Lake provided a unique evolutionary ecosystem that no other species of trout was able to penetrate. When the first whites entered the region, they found a band of peaceful Paiute Indians living almost exclusively on the giant Lahontan trout (*Salmo clarki henshawi*), which ranged in weight from forty to sixty pounds.

Lieutenant John C. Fremont, the "Great Pathfinder" of the Army Corps of Topographical Engineers, recorded the unique subspecies when he first came upon Pyramid Lake on January 10, 1844. The Indians brought the explorers great quantities of the fish—"magnificent salmon trout," wrote Charles Preuss, the expedition's cartographer. "I gorged myself until I almost choked," he wrote. Fremont himself reported that "their flavor was excellent, superior in fact, to that of any fish I have ever known. They were of extraordinary size—about as large as a Columbia River salmon—generally from two to four feet in length." The Paiutes of the region, Fremont noted, "appeared to live an easy and happy life," and they gave the white men "a salmon-trout feast as is seldom seen . . . every variety of manner in which

fish could be prepared – boiled, fried, and roasted in the ashes – was put to requisition; and every few minutes an Indian would be seen running off to spear a fresh one."

Another trout of good size that was found in local abundance was the yellowfin cutthroat (*Salmo mykiss macdonaldi*), which mysteriously was first reported in a small portion of Colorado's eastern slope about 1885. Although no one knows for certain where they came from, they thrived in Twin Lakes, near the great mining town of Leadville. The fish ranged in size from seven to ten pounds, with some reaching thirteen pounds, according to nineteenth century records.

Throughout the Platte and Arkansas river drainages in Colorado, the dainty greenback cutthroat (*Salmo clarki stomias*) abounded, while west of the divide the Colorado River cutthroat (*Salmo clarki pleuriticus*) was the ruler of aquatic domains. On the eastern slopes of the Steen and Pueblo mountains of Oregon and into Nevada, the beautiful Alvord cutthroat (*Salmo clarki alvordensis*) was found, while the Rio Grande cutthroat (*Salmo mykiss spilurus*) ranged into the canyons and gorges of the Southwest. There were other subspecies, of course, but the trout mentioned here, with the exception of the Colorado River cutthroat, all share one thing in common – today they are gone, or mostly so. The yellowfin cutthroat is probably extinct.

It was man himself who did them all in. The market fishing of the late nineteenth century and the liberal bag limits that provided for mass consumption of food fish might have been enough to do irreparable damage to these natives. But in many instances it was man's neglect coupled with his sheer desire to improve upon things that unintentionally spelled doom for the cutthroat trout. During the era of the fur trade there were scarcely enough humans living on the frontier to do everlasting damage to fish populations. But with the discovery of gold, first in California in 1848 and then in the Rocky Mountains beginning a decade later, conditions changed drastically.

Unlike the ever progressive wave of farmers pushing their way onto the frontier in an even pattern, mile by mile from east to west in a predictable fashion, the mining frontier was quite irregular. From California to Colorado and then up to the northern Rockies and finally the Southwest, miners rushed to specific locales where a gold or silver strike had been made. The result was a scattered pattern of settlements throughout the West, each hopelessly isolated at first by hundreds, sometimes thousands of wilderness miles from the nearest source of supply. There could be no reliance on established communities just a short distance to the east. Before railroads could link these isolated tent and log towns with the older, distant communities, miners were forced to be self-sufficient. Supplies of freshly killed game meat were frequently supplemented with fish from the tumbling streams.

One of the earliest fish stories on record in the Rocky Mountains occurred on February 25, 1861, in Denver City, the site three years before of the first gold strike in Kansas Territory. Isolated by hundreds of miles from civilization, the citizens of Denver had to rely primarily upon the natural resources of the region for their survival. On that winter day in 1861, the *Rocky Mountain News* reported on a "wagon load of fish" being brought in from the South Platte drainage to be sold in an open air market on Blake Street. "Think of it," marveled the *News*, "fresh fish flowing out of the canyons of the Rocky Mountains." From that time forward market fishing became a regular occupation for newly established mining camps throughout the West.

As the mining frontier grew, so did the market harvest. By the 1880s men actually made a living by supplying trout to isolated communities. A sportsman by the name of G.O. Shields, while hunting in Montana during the fall of 1884, recalled with actual admiration a market fisherman he had met in the Bitterroot Mountains:

> I know a native Bitter Rooter who, during the summer and fall of '84, fished for the market, and averaged thirty pounds a day all through the season, which he sold in Missoula at twenty-five cents a pound. . . . The market fisherman of whom I speak was a faithful devotee of the fly, and never would use any other lure. A white or gray hackle was his favorite. He used a stiff pole, about ten feet long . . . and a heavy line, with double gut [leader] for attaching the fly. He fished from the shore or waded, as was necessary to reach the best water. He cast with both hands [and] when the fish arose to the fly he was ignominiously yanked and either landed high and dry on mother earth or in the man's gunnysack. I have seen him take ten to twenty-five pounds of trout in an hour's fishing and not miss a single rise.

Ironically, it was the railroad, that great civilizing agent of the nineteenth century, that insured the success of the market fishermen. By the time railroads crossed the continent bringing to the frontier all the necessities (and luxuries) of the East, the mining industry was in a new phase. During the early years of any new mineral strike, surface metal was discovered and exploited quite rapidly. In most cases the ore, which occasionally made millionaires out of ordinary men, was deep underground in rich veins. Only heavy machinery and equally heavy capital could feasibly exploit these riches. The railroads provided both. As eastern entrepreneurs colonized the West for the purpose of exploiting its riches, great underground mines with names like the Bonanza, the Million Dollar, and the Lucky Cuss spread throughout the mountain regions. Permanent towns sprang up, their building materials supplied by the railroads. The iron horse also brought in tons of mining equipment, including dynamite to blast tunnels into the ore-rich earth. As horrible as it seems today, dynamite not only supplied the needs of the mining corporations but those of the market fishermen as well.

Although some foodstuffs could be brought in from the East by the railroad, there remained a demand for fresh meat. Supplied with a few sticks of dynamite, a market fisherman could multiply his daily harvest tenfold. The presence of the railroad, of course, expanded his market and provided him with a streamlined transportation system that enabled him to reach untapped waters. By the 1880s several western states and territories outlawed the loathsome practice of dynamiting fish, but enforcement was almost nonexistent because of the continued demand for fresh trout in many western communities. In July of 1884, a marketeer named Peter Cooper was hauled into a Denver courtroom and accused, along with his partner, of illegally dynamiting trout in the South Platte River. They got off with a verbal warning. By the next year the pair were at it again, farther south. This time, considering that it was their second offense, the court fined the men seventy-five dollars.

In mining regions like Colorado, with a substantial Chinese population, the dynamiting of fish became a particularly severe problem. Faced with a racist white society that would not allow them to start their own mines, the Chinese were forced collectively to work old claims that had been abandoned because of low yields. While waiting for such unproductive opportunities, they earned a living any way they could: as servants, launderers, and frequently, as market fishermen. Nor was the native American averse to the slaughter. After growing dependent on the white man's capitalism in order to obtain guns, utensils, and whiskey, many Indians sold trout to western communities. An 1884 issue of *Forest and Stream* reported on a band of Indians spending an entire summer on the banks of Idaho's Lake Pend Oreille dynamiting thousands of trout for sale in markets as far away as Portland, Oregon.

The demise of the cutthroat was not accomplished by market fishing alone, however. In many respects it was unintentional exploitation that took the heaviest toll. Mining and logging practices were dirty businesses, environmentally speaking. The effluents of mining wastes were carried through major waterways where they quickly devastated native cutthroats. No cutthroat trout have been reported in Clear Creek, which flows from the Colorado mining towns of Blackhawk and Central City, since the discovery of gold there in 1859.

During the last two decades of the nineteenth century, most western states and territories began to realize that a valuable resource was being rapidly decimated. Laws were enacted to protect the native cutthroats, which residents of the West categorically called "Rocky Mountain spotted trout." Enforcement was impossible, though, and many people continued to take fish in large numbers.

It is highly ironic that direct attempts to improve the quality of sport-fishing toward the end of the nineteenth century probably resulted in the destruction of more native cutthroats than all the marketeering and mining activities combined. Alarmed by the demise of the natives, town councils, sportsmen's clubs, and individuals began a frantic effort to restore fisheries in their states and territories. Game and fish commissions were established, and hatcheries were constructed to propagate trout for stocking in lakes and streams. It was such hatchery activities that led to the probable extinction of the yellowfin cutthroat in Colorado.

In 1890 a hatchery opened near Leadville for the purpose of milking the spawning yellowfins and propagating the eggs for redistribution in Twin Lakes and elsewhere. Weirs were constructed to prevent the yellowfins from migrating into the streams during the spawning season. Federal hatchery workers then captured the ripe females and milked the eggs. Local residents were furious at the practice. Historically they had been free to take the trout as the fish made their spawning runs. In many instances, Leadville citizens used pitchforks to spear the helpless spawners right on their redds, giving a macabre meaning to the term "harvest." When the annual migration of fish was stopped by the hatchery personnel, angry citizens organized posses. Shots rang out. There was at least one midnight attempt to free the fish by dynamiting the hatchery weirs. It seems that cattlemen were not the only people in the West to instigate a range war.

For about two years the hatchery propagated yellowfin eggs successfully. Then the brood stock became decimated by over-breeding. A scant ten years after the hatchery began operating, the yellowfin was gone from Twin Lakes. During the last two decades of the nineteenth century, exotic trout species, especially rainbows, were introduced into Twin Lakes from other parts of the country. Throughout the West, rainbows were planted by the millions in diminished waters. The practice spelled final doom for the native cutthroats. Being spring spawners, the rainbows readily hybridized with the natives. This process brought about the final extinction of the yellowfin trout after rainbows were planted in Twin Lakes. Everywhere in the West, rainbows quickly wiped out remnant populations of cutthroats through interbreeding. By 1900 the rainbow had replaced the cutthroat as the fish most heavily propagated in federal and state hatcheries.

Brook trout from the East, and German brown trout, were likewise introduced to western waters. Brookies spawn after attaining a size of only a few inches. Although they spawn in the fall and thus do not hybridize with cutthroats, they are, nevertheless, very prolific. In waters where they have no competition, brookies tend to be stunted, a result of overpopulation. Cutthroats simply cannot compete with the energetic brook trout.

These exotics traveled to their new Rocky Mountain homes in containers carried by the railroads. Many of the narrow-gauge lines that connected isolated mountain towns went to the extreme of offering free passage to state and federal hatchery personnel in Colorado and elsewhere. Of course the hatchery men would stock the streams and lakes adjacent to the rail lines, and then the railroad companies and the towns they served would advertise that fact to sportsmen throughout the region and even back east. Early twentieth-century booster pamphlets of the Denver & Rio Grande Railroad offered a twenty-dollar gold piece to anyone bringing in a rainbow of ten pounds or more along their right-of-way. The Gunnison River provided the action. In efforts to compete with the railroad towns, communities not linked by rail opened private hatcheries or imported exotic species from the East to plant in local waters. Throughout the first decade of the twentieth century, an advertisement ran on the back pages of *Forest and Stream*, offering for sale:

> Brook Trout of all Ages
> for stocking brooks in any quantity!
> Warranted delivery anywhere in fine condition.
> Plymouth Rock Trout Company, Plymouth, Mass.

The fish were sold to any individual or group who mailed in an order.

Even in regions where exotic species were not stocked, man's attempts to bring about progress resulted in the demise of native fish. In many ways the elimination of Pyramid Lake's giant Lahontan trout is the saddest story of all. In 1905 the Reclamation Service of the Department of the Interior built Derby Dam on the Truckee River, diverting part of the river away from Pyramid Lake for the Newlands Irrigation Project. The effects were devastating. The water level in the lake lowered dramatically. On the south end, sandbars clogged the mouth of the Truckee. The Lahontans could no longer make their annual spawning runs into the river. By 1938 they had vanished from Pyramid Lake – the entire strain was thought to be extinct. The largest trout native to western North America had been lost. Today, the trout raised under the name "Lahontan" have an entirely different genetic makeup from the former giants that composed the Pyramid Lake strain. Their average weight in Pyramid Lake today is less than twenty pounds, a weight that is half the average size of the fish reported by Fremont in 1844.

By the early twentieth century, remnant populations of cutthroats throughout the West had retreated to secretive headwater creeks deep in the high wilderness of the West's most remote mountains. There were a few exceptions of course, especially in areas of low human habitation and in regions that were spared extensive mining activity. Wyoming was one such place. With the establishment of Yellowstone National Park in 1872, hundreds of thousands of wilderness acres were set aside for preservation. Throughout this well-watered region the Yellowstone cutthroat subspecies (*Salmo clarki bouvieri*) was found in profusion. Thanks to the efforts of the National Park Service, regulations governing the Yellowstone cutthroat in its native waters are among the most strict in the nation. As a result, the fish still exist in profusion. Today, anglers from around the world travel to north-western Wyoming to fly-cast for this beautiful creature. To a lesser extent, the Snake River cutthroat (unnamed) south of the Yellowstone Plateau and the west slope cutthroat (*Salmo clarki lewisi*), the fish first seen by Lewis and Clark in 1804, likewise have made it through in pretty good shape, although pure-strain populations of the latter are rare outside Glacier National Park. These fish would not have survived if their native habitat inside the national parks and other remote areas had seen the exploitation suffered by other regions of the West.

Consequently, during the second half of the twentieth century Yellowstone and Snake River cutthroats (or hybrids of the two) have formed the core of a broodstock for raising cutthroat fry to be planted throughout the West. In fact, their ranges have actually been extended from the original distributions. But in many cases the transplanted

strains are not genetically pure. They still interbreed with other cutthroats and with rainbows in waters where the two species are found.
As a result they are generally planted only in remote waters, sometimes by airplane. And that is where I purposefully seek them out
every summer.

Shortly after ice out I make my annual treks to wilderness lakes,
high on the continental divide. If I'm lucky the fishing can be fantastic. At times the cruising fish will take any offering I present, although
a #14 Zug Bug or a small Hare's Ear nymph fished just under the surface seem to be the most consistent producers. Stealth is necessary
when the fish are feeding in the shallows (it's more hunting than fishing), and I've found that windy, rainy days are more productive than
sunny ones, although there have been some remarkable exceptions.

Now, I don't claim to be a scientist, and to my untrained eye one
cutthroat looks pretty much like the next. The distinctive crimson
slashes outside and below the lower jaws, which account for this fish's
common name, are present in all subspecies. I know that the Yellowstone variety is supposed to have large spots concentrated toward the
posterior while the Snake River subspecies has more and blacker spots.
In Colorado the Colorado River cutthroat is widely planted, and I
don't even know what it's "supposed" to look like. But given the
genetic impurity of most of these fish I usually can't tell one from
the other. It makes no difference really; like most people, if I don't
know the strain for certain I just call them "natives." In many locales
a cutthroat is a cutthroat and it's a pretty rare fish. I believe any cutthroat, genetically pure or otherwise, deserves to be released. The fact
that I catch a Wyoming native in Colorado waters has no bearing on
my decision not to kill a fish, though I must admit it's really special
to catch and release pure-strain cutts in their native habitat when I
know for certain they are present. Up until a few years ago, however,
that scenario was unlikely outside Yellowstone and a few other areas.
But, now, thanks to some forward-looking scientists, the situation
has changed.

Since the late 1960s some cutthroat subspecies have been "rediscovered"; the reason?—people have actively looked for them. In 1984
biologists with the Nevada Department of Wildlife caught some unusual looking cutthroats in the headwaters of Virgin Creek. The fish
were determined to be alvords—thought to be long extinct. They will
now be protected and propagated in an effort to extend their range.

In 1977 a graduate student discovered pure-strain Pyramid Lake cut-throats in a small creek along the Utah-Nevada border. There is even hope that the yellowfin trout might one day be found, perhaps over-seas, where eggs were shipped during the 1890s. But to me the most remarkable story of all is the rediscovery of the greenback cutthroat.

The greenback was the only trout native to the Platte and Arkan-sas drainages along the eastern slope of Colorado. Located adjacent to the Rocky Mountain West's largest population centers, the fishery was especially vulnerable. The greenback's decline was swift, and the subspecies was thought to be completely extinct by the 1930s. But in 1969 a few pure-strain greenbacks were discovered in Como Creek, a small mountain brook near my home in Boulder, Colorado. A natu-ral barrier on the creek apparently kept brook trout from migrating upstream, thus the greenbacks survived. Sixty of these trout were col-lected, and fifty-two of them were transplanted into a place called Black Hollow near Fort Collins in order to enlarge their range. By the late 1970s the finicky spawners were being propagated at the federal hatch-ery in Bozeman, Montana, for reintroduction to Colorado waters.

Today, the greenback has been successfully transplanted into sev-eral locations in Rocky Mountain National Park through the coura-geous efforts of a group known as the Greenback Recovery Team. Reintroduction has required cleaning out other fish, especially brook trout, through the use of environmentally safe chemical poison. Fish barriers have been constructed in several locations to keep other trout from moving upstream and intermingling with the greenbacks. The program has been such a success that the greenback cutthroat has been downgraded by the federal government from "endangered" to "threat-ened." This reclassification has resulted in the opening of certain green-back waters to strictly regulated angling with artificial flies and lures on single, barbless hooks. Fishing is on a catch-and-release basis. From 1982–1986 several high-country creeks and lakes have been opened. Beginning in 1986 the greenback was reintroduced into the Arkansas River drainage, and plans for further expansion are in the works.

I remember well catching my first greenback. It was in a string of beaver ponds located along a main road in Rocky Mountain Na-tional Park. The Federal Wildlife Service encouraged fishing there to eliminate the brookies that somehow had reestablished themselves in the ponds. The idea was to release all cutthroats and keep the brook-ies, some of which were quite large. Many anglers found it difficult to kill these nice brookies while releasing the smaller greenbacks. To the consternation of wildlife officials, many of the brookies were also released, and some of them are still there. On my first outing I caught no brook trout, but I had a field day with the greenbacks.

My first fish came to a dry fly. I came up on the pond from the downstream side, being very careful to keep a low profile and stay far enough away so as not to cast a shadow on the water. The surface was crystal clear. I could see trout cruising near the surface whenever the sun ducked behind an afternoon cloud. When it would reappear, the dimpling of fish on the surface of the pond would temporarily cease. I tied a #20 Adams onto a twelve-foot leader tapered to 7X and waited patiently for the sun to go behind a cloud once again. Finally the perfect moment was at hand. I false casted three times and then laid down a short, gentle cast to the tail of the pond, just above the beaver dam where the water spilled into the channel where I was standing.

Immediately a greenback rose and hit the Adams with authority. I raised the rod tip slightly and began playing the fish. I knew immediately that the trout was small. Moments later I held it gently in my hand, a whopping nine-incher. At that moment, however, it was the most beautiful trout I had ever seen. It wasn't because it fought hard—it didn't. And it wasn't because the fish was large—it was not (I understand that greenbacks seldom exceed twelve inches). It wasn't because the fish looked different. It looked pretty much the same as any other cutthroat (remember: I can't tell the difference between them). I guess it was magnificent simply because it came from out of the past—and because it had *survived*. In the few seconds that I held the fish, my subconscious mind told me that this was the trout the founders of my community had known, the only trout they had known.

The ancestors of this very fish had sustained early settlers in the Boulder Valley; it fed the miners of Gold Hill and Wallstreet. It was known to the English traveler Isabella Bird in 1873, and she described it as a "speckeled Beauty" in her classic *A Lady's Life in the Rocky Mountains*. The Earl of Dunraven had fished for it on his enormous private preserve in Estes Park. But more importantly, the ancestors of this fish had been sold by the wagonload on Blake Street in Denver during the 1860s and 1870s. It had been dynamited and poisoned by mining wastes throughout most of its native waters during the 1880s. And yet it had survived, survived the growth of a mighty metropolis and the development of one of the greatest outdoor recreational playgrounds in the world during the twentieth century. Now I held it in my hand, a relic of the past; only a vestige of that bygone era to be sure, but the presence of this fish was nothing short of miraculous considering the enormous odds against it.

Very gently I released the trout. It shot off to safety in the black water depths of the beaver pond. My hand trembled ever so slightly at that moment, and I didn't mind a bit that this particular fish was not a three-pound rainbow from a world-famous river.

Fishing the Diminished Wilderness

One thing we westerners have always had to face is tourists. They are as much a part of our environment as dry weather and russet sunsets. Tourists are the logical extension of the great westward expansion into the twentieth century.

In the majority of the western states, tourism is the most important regional industry. And in most of the Rocky Mountain states, hunting, fishing, and other outdoor recreational pursuits represent the most important element of that tourist industry. But many of us blame "the tourists" for everything from fluctuations in the economy to the declining numbers of big trout. That's nothing new. The West has a long tradition of encouraging tourism, and for years westerners have been complaining about it.

Originally, of course, just about everyone was a "greenhorn" in the West (even the native Americans if you go back far enough). But after the initial settlements in California and Colorado, following the discovery of gold, tourists and part-time residents started showing up in the West in remarkable numbers, especially during the summer months. By the late 1860s, the high, dry air of the Rockies was widely prescribed by physicians throughout the country as a tonic for tuberculosis and other chronic respiratory ailments. Soon, fashionable sanitoriums sprang up at the base of the mountains to cater to the every need of wealthy eastern consumptives. The city of Colorado Springs owes its existence to these elegant spas. For the less affluent, however, a tent or crude log cabin among the pine and aspen was home for as much as six months of the year. They came by the thousands, these unfortunates, to partake of the "camp cure." Most of them would summer along the bank of a sparkling trout stream where an ample catch of fish would keep them in fresh meat. Unfortunately, some of these early tourists even fished for the market in order to obtain needed cash for provisions during their extended stays. The newspapers were full of reports blaming the market harvest on "outsiders."

It is hard to say how much impact these consumptives had on trout populations or the development of the angling sport in the West. Certainly, many of them decided to move west permanently, and in significant ways, some of them enriched the culture and the natural environment of the region to a considerable degree. Enos Mills was one of the sufferers who did just that. Emigrating to Colorado from Kansas in 1884, Mills became obsessed with preserving the natural environment of Colorado's great peaks and forests around Estes Park. Chiefly through his efforts, Rocky Mountain National Park was created on September 4, 1915, thus preserving forever miles of alpine lakes, streams, and forests once exploited unmercifully by the Earl of Dunraven and others.

Of course many tuberculosis victims eventually returned to their homes in the East, where they told stories to their neighbors about the wonders of the West. The transcontinental railroad was completed in 1869, and by the 1870s bona fide vacationers were starting to appear in increasing numbers. The West would never be the same again. By the 1880s hundreds of miles of spur lines and narrow-gauge railroads linked up with the main east to west routes. With great rapidity the tourist could be transported in luxury to most of the great trout water in the West. At the turn of the century, a trip of only a few hours from Denver could get a visiting angler (not to mention citizens of Denver) onto the famous Frying Pan River via the Colorado Midland Railroad. A few hours more on one of these special "fish trains," and the same fly-fisher could be testing the waters of the Gunnison after a scenic trip on the Denver and Rio Grande. Many of these intermountain lines advertised the fabulous fishing to be had along their routes, even offering prizes for the biggest fish caught each month. The wilderness shrank steadily during the great era of railroad building.

State and territorial governments added to the attraction by publishing pamphlets, or encouraging the publication of such among local businessmen, to attract both tourists and new residents. This "booster literature" accomplished the purpose of attracting people, but often at the expense of the environment. By the early 1900s many of the natural resources had become scarce; booster literature had not. In the June 15, 1912, issue of *Forest and Stream*, an angler by the name of N.H. Hilton urged tourists to come out and fish in Wyoming's Big Horn Mountains:

> It is no trick to get seventy-five to a hundred trout in a day, and they will average eleven to twelve inches. They sure are some fighters.
>
> The rivers can be waded at any point, and are easily fished. We use four- to six-ounce rods about nine or ten feet long; and for flies, my book contains, after much experience, the royal coachman, professor, white-miller, cow-dung, gray hackle, queen-of-the-waters and the stone fly, and I have them all made with a No. 3 sneck hook.
>
> My record last year for speed was seven trout in nine minutes with a royal coachman fly. The trout were all over twelve inches.
>
> There is no closed season for trout in Wyoming, which shows that we have plenty.

Not to be outdone, the governor of Colorado, John F. Shafroth, wrote an article for *Forest and Stream* that very summer proclaiming his state to possess superior trout fishing for visiting tourists. He assured vacationers that:

> The streams are annually stocked by both the Game and Fish Department of the State of Colorado, and the Federal Government. The state in 1911 put 11,000,000 trout fry into the streams, the output of the various State fish hatcheries. The output for 1912 will be about 14,000,000 fry, insuring a continuous supply of the speckled beauties. Tourists intending coming to Colorado for pleasure will find inviting accommodations and camping grounds along any of the streams where beautiful scenery and fine fishing will be found.

With large limits in the western states and territories and fast railroads to get them there, tourists came by the thousands during the early years of the twentieth century. When local anglers of the early twentieth century found the fishing to be poor, they blamed the tourists. But the boostering in the popular press went on, sometimes unrealistically. It is arguable that this capitalistically motivated yellow journalism, in respect to all aspects of western life, did more to mythicize the region than any other single factor.

The onslaught on Yellowstone began shortly after national park status was conferred in 1872. During Yellowstone's first decade, tourists were several days' ride from the nearest towns and railheads.

Wonderland was an isolated and somewhat dangerous place to visit. But despite its forbidding reputation, the tourists still came in modest numbers to camp and fish even in the park's earliest years, although not without incident. In at least one notable case, visiting sportsmen camped in the park were actually captured by Indians.

In the year 1877, when primitive Yellowstone National Park was barely five years old, the peaceful Nez Perce who had lived in the Wallowa Valley of northeastern Oregon since before the Great Treaty of 1855, which "guaranteed" them legal rights to these lands, were forced to accept a smaller reservation.

A misunderstanding between a few Nez Perce braves who did not wish to leave their homeland and some white settlers resulted in the deaths of the white homesteaders and the start of another Indian war. The Nez Perce, under the guidance of Chief Joseph, decided to cross the Rockies and join the Sioux in Canada. Thus began a most remarkable exodus which scarcely has its parallel in American history. During the short summer months, the Nez Perce, including women, children, the sick, and the elderly, traveled a distance of almost 1700 miles over rugged terrain, defending themselves from federal troops under the command of General O.O. Howard at almost every step. Back east, some citizens were pulling for the Nez Perce to make it all the way to Canada as they followed their journey in the newspapers. They almost made it. In fact, about 330 actually escaped across the border. Over 400, however, surrendered when General Nelson A. Miles cut them off near the Bear Paw Mountains, almost within sight of the Canadian border.

During their journey eastward, one of the most bizarre events in the annals of the Indian wars occurred. Interestingly, the route of Joseph and his people paralleled some of the most famous trout streams in America. From the vicinity of Idaho's Henry's Lake, the Indians crossed Targhee Pass into the Madison Valley, where they followed that river right into Yellowstone National Park, through where the town of West Yellowstone and the west entrance to the park are now located. They moved up the Firehole and eventually crossed the Yellowstone River itself. When the Nez Perce crossed the park boundary, there were approximately nine parties of tourists totaling at least thirty-five people camped in various locations. We cannot verify for certain that any of them were trout fishing, but it seems highly probable. One of the parties, in fact, included the Earl of Dunraven and his English friend, the novelist Charles Kingsley. Dunraven is known to have fished the Yellowstone River during his escapades in the West (they even named one of the park's mountain passes after him), and it is likely that he was doing so when word spread around the camp that the Nez Perce were in the park.

The Indians captured a lone camper named John Shivley on the East Fork of the Firehole River (now called Nez Perce Creek) and forced him to guide them through the unfamiliar park (he later escaped). Most of the tourists (including Dunraven), when they became aware of the Indians' presence, attempted to congregate at a crude hotel being operated at Mammoth Hot Springs. The so-called "Radersburg party," however, was less fortunate. These nine campers found themselves directly in the path of the Indians and were captured. Many of the Indians were kind to the members of the Radersburg party and another party of tourists who were later encountered. Other young warriors, who perhaps had lost family or friends at the Battle of the Big Hole, were not. A few of these angry young warriors wanted to kill the whites. In fact, a few were killed by the more impassioned warriors of the tribe.

Of those shot by the Indians, few were as lucky as one man by the name of George Cowan. Now I have slipped down hillsides—even mountainsides—on my way to a trout stream. I've fallen in the water innumerable times, cut my hands open, executed involuntary somersaults over deadfalls, been caught in the wilderness without toilet paper, scraped my knees, skinned my face, sliced my fanny, and pulled hooks from my ear lobes, but I have never had as harrowing an encounter as this poor tourist, George Cowan. After his capture and a ten-mile forced march, one angry brave rode up to him and shot him in the right leg. Another warrior then proceeded to place a bullet squarely in the middle of his forehead.

But Cowan lived. Apparently the gun of the second warrior either partially misfired or was an old cap-and-ball weapon loaded with a weak charge. The bullet half protruded from Cowan's head. He got up and began to hobble with the aid of a branch. Unfortunately, yet another warrior spotted him and shot him in the left leg. Cowan played dead, and the Indian rode on. Now he began to crawl, and crawl, and then crawl some more—for four long days and nights and about ten miles. Finally, he made it back to his old campsite at Madison Junction. The others in the party had been taken away by the Nez Perce (they were later released). With the bullet still sticking out of his forehead, Cowan brewed himself a cup of coffee and sat up to drink it. There he was finally discovered by two men carrying supplies to Fort Fisher. They only wrapped him in a couple of blankets and rode on. The next day he was discovered by General Howard's troops.

But Cowan's ordeal wasn't over. Apparently, the Army surgeons didn't think his affliction that severe, for according to Cowan's later testimony, the physicians were more interested in "sightseeing in the geyser basin" than tending his wounds. The bullet still protruded from his forehead, squarely above the nose. Finally, he was treated and taken to the Yellowstone River, where he was put on a wagon train on its way to Bozeman. On this seventy-mile journey, the wagon Cowan was in slid over an embankment, throwing the patient into a deep gully. When he finally reached civilization and the apparent safety of a hospital bed, one side of the bed frame collapsed, spilling Cowan, once again, onto the hard ground. At this point he allegedly remarked, "Why don't they bring on the artillery; they've tried everything else!" I do not know if his unfortunate experience was ever published in a "This Happened to Me" column of a major sporting journal, but Cowan returned to camp and fish in the park in later years. Not even such a harrowing ordeal could keep this tourist from returning to the West's greatest playground.

By the late 1890s Yellowstone was a much safer place, and the increase in tourism during the Gay Nineties reflected that fact. Tourists could reach the general vicinity via the Northern Pacific Railroad and then make the trip into the park by stage. Affluent Victorians from around the world came to sample the fishing in Yellowstone waters. Charles E. Brooks, writing in *The Living River* (1979), tells the tale of a blooded English sportsman named Sir Rose Lambert Price who had become so enchanted with the old stories of the mountain men of the Yellowstone catching trout and cooking them in the fishing cone without the necessity of taking them off the hook that he decided to perpetuate the tradition. Price tried to match the same feat utilizing the thermal pools of the Firehole River. He wrote:

> I had not time at Yellowstone Lake to try from the fishing cone there, to catch and boil a trout without removing it from the hook, or touching it with the hand, and here was a chance of performing so unique a feat. . . . More line and a longer cast to take me beyond the water already flogged, and flop, whirr, I am well struck into a game pounder. . . . I got him under control at last. Fortunately the cast was a strong one, and working him up to the edge of the crater,

one strong pull on a short line dropped him into the boiling water
and the feat was accomplished.

Eighteen years later, in 1915, private automobiles became legal in
Yellowstone National Park. The railroad from Ogden, Utah, had already reached the west entrance in June of 1909. The horse and buggy
days were over, and so was the era of few tourists. Visitors to the park
doubled, tripled, and then tripled again within a few short years. The
quality of the fishing declined proportionately.

It is almost impossible to underestimate the impact that Henry
Ford and his colleagues had on the tourist industry in the U.S., especially on the West's "playgrounds." The initial popularity of the
automobile coincided with the establishment of many of the West's
national parks. When Rocky Mountain was dedicated in 1915, for example, dignitaries rode to the ceremonies in autos. F.O. Stanley, the
inventor of the Stanley Steamer, was a resident of Estes Park and was
present at the ceremony, symbolizing, in retrospect, the dawn of a
new age in tourist transportation. The railroad had been revolutionary, to be sure; it was even partially responsible for the demise of trout
resources in the West. But it was *nothing* like the automobile.

During the great age of steam, pristine valleys still existed where
beautiful mountain streams would yield huge trout that had never
before seen an artificial fly. Vast expanses of rangelands and mountains were unscarred by auto roads at the dawn of the twentieth century. Sportsmen could still spend several days in the saddle, or riding
in a rickety buckboard, in search of prime water. But the automobile
changed all that. Dirt roads were cheaper to construct than railroads,
and as automobiles became more numerous and reliable, tourism to
western destinations mushroomed. The quality of trout fishing diminished correspondingly.

The decrease in bag limits coincided directly with the increase in
cars. By the 1920s, a twenty-fish limit had been imposed. It was steadily reduced as more tourists visited the park each summer. Shortly after
World War II it was down to five fish per day, and by the 1960s, catch-
and-release regulations started to be imposed. It is from that decade
forward that park fishing started to improve dramatically.

The automobile, of course, opened up vast areas of the former
frontier during the twentieth century that had never been reached by
rail and were still relatively pristine. This was especially true in the

Southwest. In 1900 New Mexico was the most culturally remote region in the U.S. Its connection to the rest of the country was the great Santa Fe Railroad, perhaps the most enterprising of all American rail lines in developing tourism in the U.S. Its name is synonymous with the "opening" of New Mexico and Arizona. Closely associated with the Santa Fe Railroad after the turn of the century was the remarkable business enterprise founded by Fred Harvey. Originally a restaurant enterprise that provided food at the Santa Fe station stops, by the 1920s the company had become the hottest tourist concern in the country. Its mastermind was a retired British Army officer by the name of Major R. Hunter Clarkson. Clarkson combined the idea of linking rail transportation with automobile travel for purposes of sightseeing and recreation.

Passengers would disembark at Santa Fe depots throughout the Southwest and then be whisked away in elegant Packard touring cars to view Indian dances at the Taos Pueblo or to climb the ladders of ancient ruins at Bandelier, Chaco Canyon, or Mesa Verde. Articulate young coeds, adorned in high boots and lavish squash blossom necklaces, were hired as "couriers" to guide the tourists and answer every question they might have (such as, "Where's the best fishing?").

The automobile also brought fishermen to the Southwest for the first time in large numbers. One major trout stream near Santa Fe was, and still is, the Pecos River. For centuries the pastoral Hispanic villagers of the upper Pecos Valley had kept the cultural and environmental integrity of the region pretty well intact. Rio Grande cutthroats, some big ones, still called the Pecos home. In 1890 a fly-fisher by the name of John Carnifex fished the Pecos and reported in the July 1891 issue of *Outing Magazine* that "As to the trout, there is no end to them, all the way up to the patriarchal five pounders." Carnifex recommended bringing a rather eclectic assortment of eastern flies, including "Royal Coachmen, cowdung, brown hackle, cock-a-bondhu, Seth Green, and professor" tied on #9 hooks. Things were to change soon. Carnifex fished the Pecos many years later (after tourists had rediscovered it) and complained that the trout in the river had diminished in size.

The famous Taos artist Ernest Blumenschein frequently would leave his studio on Ledoux Street to fish the Rio Grande or the Pecos. On one bright August day in 1929, "Blumy" caught a large brown trout that enchanted him so much he returned to his studio to paint a picture of it on the door. His daughter Helen is still living in Taos, and during a recent conversation with her, she could not remember how long the fish actually was, but she invited me to come down and measure its portrait. I intend to do so. Blumenschein and his associates in the Taos Society of Artists, of course, along with the likes of D.H. Lawrence, Georgia O'Keeffe, and the former darling of New York salon society, Mabel Dodge Luhan, were some of the big attractions for huge numbers of tourists during the early years of the twentieth century. New Mexico was the nation's most popular tourist destination during the '20s, and the small Pecos River received its first real onslaught of visiting fishermen in its history during this time.

Even before the Harvey cars started rolling, eastern tourists were beginning to show up in New Mexico in their private automobiles. In 1917 Florence M. Pettee made the trip to the Pecos from "three-quarters of a continent away." The remarkable journey by roadster for that day and age was such a sensation that her story was published as a feature article on the pages of *Forest and Stream* in July 1918. Many of the Anglo tourists who visited New Mexico in these early decades of the twentieth century were unfamiliar with the native American and Hispanic cultures of the area. Consequently, their behavior and written accounts are threaded with patronization and paternalism (New Mexico didn't attain statehood until 1914 chiefly due to racist prejudices held by some members of Congress toward the predominant non-Anglo population). In such an isolated, sparsely populated land it is natural to assume that many visiting sport-fishers of the early twentieth century still regarded natural resources, including trout, as being untapped and unlimited. Florence Pettee did. Witness the title of her article: "The Paradise of all Trout Fishermen; The Upper Pecos, Where the West is Nowhere Wilder and Where A Meal Lies A-Basking and Awaiting the Mere Casting of a Bait."

The Pettee party stayed at a weathered adobe ranch in the valley where they were supplied with "the proper species of Mexican trout flies," which resembled "red-bodied mosquitoes." After a cooling desert thunderstorm, and with a distinct fragrance of pinon smoke and wet adobe hanging in the valley, the party rigged up their "bamboo fly rods" and went fishing. The roads up the valley were merely dirt trails, and Hispanic sheepherders could be seen crossing the stream on their burros, for there were few bridges in 1917. Florence Pettee caught two big trout of several pounds each. The others in the party had equal success. Condescendingly, in relation to the part of the country she was fishing, Pettee referred to her two large trout as "Heap Big Chief number one" and "Heap Big Chief number two." Consider this account of what many fly-fishers circa 1917 considered to be a rightful and logical conclusion to a successful fishing trip:

> Heap Big Chief [number 2] was dressed first, and rolled in meal with half a dozen other relatives who quickly followed. Our camping grate was impaled in the [stream] bank and soon the blazing wood was replaced by glowing coals. The grate held troughs in which the dabs of butter flowed down merrily while the trout roasted quickly and a delicious aroma penetrated the air. Shortly the delectable morsels

were transferred to enamel plates and with bread and butter supple-
menting a tin cup of coffee hot from the bottle, made quite the
memorable feast of a memorable journey.

Today, the population of wild brown trout in the Pecos is healthy,
but the fish run small. The rainbows are mostly stockers. Both the
browns and rainbows average under twelve inches. In 1972 I hiked
into the wilderness headwaters of this stream on a three-day backpack
trip. The fish up there were wilder and a bit more numerous, but
certainly not any larger.

In the 1980s automobiles are more numerous and reliable than they
ever have been. Most families, including mine, own at least two. And
fishing, especially fly-fishing, has never been more popular than it is
today. On the Yellowstone, the Madison, or for that matter even on
the Pecos, you are likely to encounter anglers from any of the fifty
states or Canada with a smattering of foreign tourists thrown in for
good measure. Fortunately, management policies are more enlightened than in the days when anglers would roll their "heap big chiefs"
in corn meal and roast them on the stream bank. The fly-fishing boom
has had a lot to do with that. Sure, I see a few "game hogs" now and
then. I even fish with a few friends who make a habit of killing their
limits where regulations permit.

But for the most part, the new generation of fly-fishers is more
enlightened about the cause of conservation than at any time before
in our history. Certainly I might meet a guy from Pennsylvania who
will argue the fine points of exact dry mayfly imitation and who dis-
dains the techniques of certain forms of western nymph and streamer
fishing. He might look at my heavily weighted "South Platte" nymphing rig, complete with dropper and #10 Royal Wulff dry fly as strike
indicator, and accuse me of not being a *real* fly-fisherman. But I would
rather meet that sort of a person than one who breaks the law, abuses
the environment, or "fishes out" the stream.

More and more it is becoming fashionable to limit your kill, and
that trend knows no geographical or cultural boundaries. There is no
East versus West–no tourist versus native, when both demonstrate
the same respect for conserving trout resources in waters where limited-
kill regulations can truly increase the size and numbers of wild trout.
I recently saw a documentary piece put together by one of those slick
weekly news shows on network television. Hugh Downs introduced
a family containing two generations of New York physicians who were

visiting the Yellowstone River for the first time to fish with Bud Lilly. After the younger doctor in the party caught a nice trout, he kissed it goodbye before release. He said something to the effect that "you really gotta love 'em to kiss 'em on the lips like that." I'll have to attribute that quirk to the good doctor's training in his vocation rather than his avocation—I've never been one to kiss trout on the lips, but I do understand the man's romance. He understands the sport. He is in harmony with the wild environment and the beautiful creature we call the trout, which enriches and renews our lives each spring.

On some western trout rivers today, the fishing pressure is as great as anywhere in the U.S. But despite the increasing influx of angler-tourists to the West and a growing interest in the sport in general, that kind of sportsman will always be welcome on western waters. The quality of fishing will only improve because of his presence. And if I happen to get in an argument over tactics with one of these guys? Well—let's just call that a minor difference of opinion between a couple of fraternal fly-fishers.

The Museum:
A Yellowstone Reverie

An impervious gray mist shrouded the valley that morning, ghost-like. Long tendrils of the fog deliberately penetrated the forest on the far riverbank and clung tightly to the branches of the tallest pines. The air was cloying. A pair of green-winged teal peeled around a far bend in the river and darted silently above me in the dense morning light. Cold weather had moved in the previous evening. My calendar showed me it was August, but time can get lost in these woods. In a sense it is meaningless. I just *felt* it would snow.

"Never mind that," I told myself. "You have traveled over great distances, through rolling prairie and endless sagebrush flats to reach this fabled cutthroat river. Already there is a big trout down there in that hole with one of your good flies stuck in his jaw. A spate of bad weather is not going to drive you back to camp."

No insects were on the water, however. The anticipated hatch had not come off in the cooler air. Consequently, I was fishing a tiny Pheasant-Tail nymph, size 18, with three split shot pinched on about a foot above the fly. The winter snowpack had been light that year up on Two Ocean Plateau, and the river was low. I could see trout everywhere in the riffles, endless pods of fish. They schooled up in the riffles. I cast my line into the riffles and watched for approaching trout in the clear water. The strike, when it came, was not the subtle "bump" I expected. I had no need for a strike indicator.

I knew, from the previous fish, that I dare not touch my line when the trout seized the nymph. Consequently, my rod did not bend over double. I felt no wracking jolt vibrate through the cork grip of the nine-foot Orvis graphite. No—the line simply stripped out twenty feet in a split second. I first knew the fish was on not by feeling it, but by hearing it, as the spool on my old Hardy reel literally buzzed and hummed when the big trout made its first of several runs. Very gently, I palmed the reel spool. The fish slowed. I raised the tip slowly. And that was when the rod nearly bent over double. The tippet held. The trout was well hooked.

Suddenly it made another rush downstream. I was almost into the backing. Then the fish turned and torpedoed straight toward me. I climbed onto dry land and frantically stripped in line to maintain tension. A few seconds later, the big cutt shot back downstream toward a deep hole. There it sulked as I tried to "horse" it out of the hole, not wishing to dangerously exhaust it. My pulse raced. Just

downstream from the deep hole were some long, swift rapids. If the
fish ran from the hole into the fast whitewater, there would be no
way my tippet could withstand the battering. I maintained a steady
tension. The muscles in my arm began to ache.

I was lucky. The fish had tired. Slowly and repeatedly, I pumped
the rod and brought the trout to net. I quickly measured it—just a
shade over eighteen inches, but plump, well muscled, and firm. It
was a female. I turned out the hook and revived the cutthroat gently.
Finally, it shot away from my grasp with a splash from its tail. Then
I felt an adrenaline rush—not the heart-wrenching kind of rush that
you get when the fish first seizes the fly, but the satisfying kind of
rush you get from a job well done. It would have been fitting if someone's philharmonic orchestra could have struck up some classic can-
tata at that moment (Schiller's "Ode to Joy" from Beethoven's Ninth
Symphony comes to mind). I didn't care if I caught any more fish
that morning. The goal had been accomplished. By late afternoon of
that chilly day, I was tired and sore. I returned to camp for a good
meal and a night's sleep. There had been no snow. Before I turned
in for the night, however, I recorded in my fishing log that I had struck
over seventy-five trout and landed in the vicinity of thirty-five. The
fish ran between fourteen and nineteen inches in length. I also noted
that I lost or broke off "too many."

Now, I'm quite sure many of you could guess, even without reading the title of this chapter, that I was fishing the Yellowstone River,
inside the national park, above the upper falls. It's not surprising—
not even unusual. Taking fifty trout of that size or greater in a single
day on the Yellowstone is not uncommon. What you might find surprising, however, is the journal entry I read the week after I returned
home from that trip. It was written by an angler fishing the same spot
I had worked all that day. The entry read:

> At 4:30 o'clock I stopped fishing, having landed thirty-five trout,
> which would run from two and a half to four and a half pounds in
> weight . . . and I must have struck from seventy-five to one hundred
> of these immense fish. I am sure I lost more than I landed.

As I mentioned, the man was fishing the same spot as I. He even
noted that, "hundreds of trout could be seen swimming and darting
swiftly up and down the current, but near the bottom." I had observed that wonderful sight too. They were the same trout—sort of;

Yellowstone cutthroats (*Salmo clarki bouvieri*), wild fish, and very close to being genetically pure. Both that man and I had used a rod made by the same manufacturer, Orvis. What's more, that man and I were even fishing during the same week of the same month. A few of the man's fish were slightly larger than mine, but aside from that, our experiences were almost identical. "So what?" you say. "That stretch of river supports an average of 4500 anglers per mile during the season. Lots of guys have the same experience. What's the point?"

Here's the point. The other guy fished that same spot, almost to the day, 110 years before me. And in terms of numbers, size (almost), genetic makeup of the fish, and our angling success—nothing was much different than it was over a century ago. That story is almost astounding considering that these parallel escapades took place in one of the most heavily traveled (and fished) tourist spots in the world, and I dare any dedicated Maine fly-fisher of the fabled Rangeley Lakes, who knows how fabulous the fishing was there a century ago, to match it.

Actually, of course, much change did take place during the past century. By the 1960s the cutthroats in the Yellowstone averaged only between ten and twelve inches. But through what has to be one of the most enlightened and successful wildlife management programs in history, the size and numbers of trout in the Yellowstone are approaching their nineteenth-century glory. Considering that the trout in this river are not exotics, but the original strain of natives, the story is all the more remarkable. Perhaps there are similar waters somewhere in the lower forty-eight states where you can consistently catch sixteen-inch, *true* native trout in pristine conditions only a few steps from your car—but I sure don't know about them.

In any event, the Yellowstone for me is special. All things considered (including genetic subspecies of the fish), it is the only river I know of where a good fly-fisher can easily sample what trout fishing in the West was like over a century ago—if you don't mind a little companionship on the river, that is. Often, conditions can be quite crowded. Miraculously, though, all seem to catch their share of fish on a good day. But aside from that great reality of the automobile age, the Yellowstone experience is, truly, living history.

The political and social history of the region is rich and varied, but I am much more concerned with the history of fishing in the river itself. Suffice it to say that during the era of the Rocky Mountain fur trade, the superstitious Indians of the region stayed out of the geyser-laden area, making it a haven for the mountain men.

Beginning in 1870, a series of military and scientific expeditions were sent into the region to ascertain the truth about the thermal phenomena, which were regarded by many in Washington and throughout the East as merely a product of the imaginations of the storytelling fur trappers. The first of these important explorations was the famous Washburn-Doane Expedition of 1870. One of the civilian members of that expedition was a pioneer Montana merchant from the Helena area named Warren C. Gillette. He kept a meticulous diary of the historic trip. On the morning of August 28, the party was camped near the river in the vicinity of the Sulphur Cauldron. Gillette went down to the river to do some fishing. Later in the day he recorded in his journal that he "caught 7 fine trout that would weigh from 2 to 2-1/2 pounds each. These fish," Gillette claimed, "were not gamy like the trout of the East. They make but little resistance in being taken from the water & do not run with the hook after taking the bait."

Thus, Warren Gillette became one of the first whites to "officially" catch the big cutthroats of the Yellowstone (at least one member of his party even fished with flies). His report also inaugurated one of the bigger controversies regarding the gaming quality of these fish; an argument that is still persistent in fly-fishing circles today. In fact many of the local guides claim they won't fish the Yellowstone because the fish are too easy to catch and are sluggish on the hook. They much prefer the fighting rainbows of the Madison River. I have not made up my own mind regarding this issue. At times I have hooked sixteen-inchers that seem to roll over within a minute or so, sulking on the bottom and almost never breaking water like a rainbow. At other times, however, I have hooked fourteen-inchers that have taken me many yards downstream in their runs, and fight as well as any trout of that size I have ever caught.

Later in the season, when the fish have been hooked and released several times, their selectiveness can become as challenging as any fly-fisher could hope for. In addition, I am convinced that these late-season trout have been caught so many times that they have acquired the habits of quail when heavily pushed. That is, they have predetermined a deep hole, rapids, or other suitable hiding place, and when hooked, nothing short of an earthquake measuring 7.5 on the Richter

scale is going to deter them from running into that sanctuary. A day
of fishing for these trout can send many an angler to the local drug-
store for a bottle of liniment to treat his aching arm muscles. In any
event, the reputation these fish have for sluggishness may actually be
more of a blessing than a curse. Extensive research has concluded that
the survival rate after release of these Yellowstone cutthroats is among
the highest anywhere. Perhaps that is because they do not dangerously exhaust themselves because they have "learned" that they will
be released.

In 1874 the Earl of Dunraven wrote extensively about his fishing
experiences on the river and proclaimed the sport on the Yellowstone
to be the finest he had ever encountered. In 1875, an unusual military
expedition entered the new Yellowstone National Park. The entourage was headed by Grant's secretary of war, General William Worth
Belknap. General Randolph Barnes Marcy, a hopelessly addicted fly-
fisherman and inspector general of the army, was with the group as
was General James William Forsyth, an officer on General Phillip Sheridan's staff. The official chronicler of the expedition was General William Strong of Chicago, the only noncareer officer of the group.

When these men reached the West, they were joined by Lieutenant Gustavus C. Doane, General Nelson Bowman Sweitzer, Colonel
George L. Gillespie, and no less than twenty-four enlisted men, some
of whom served as orderlies. Including noncommissioned officers, the
party consisted of thirty-five men. One can speculate that the trip may
have been the last truly pleasant experience Secretary Belknap ever
had. Less than six months after his return to Washington, he was
accused of malfeasance in his office and unanimously impeached by
the House of Representatives; quite an embarrassment (among many)
for President Grant.

In any event, Belknap masterminded the expedition to assert the
U.S. Army's concern that the game resources of Yellowstone National
Park were being destroyed because of the administrative ineptness of
the Department of the Interior, which at that time supervised the
park. These men, who had witnessed the destruction of the buffalo
and the threatened extinction of other big game, were, by their own
convoluted definition, "conservationists." In accordance with the mid-
nineteenth-century concept of conservation, these affluent bureau-
crats exhibited the double standard common to much of the thought
at that time regarding fish and game management. Like the Earl of

Dunraven and others, these men bemoaned the exploitations of market hunters and fishers on the one hand, while on the other advocated the preservation of wild areas for the unregulated pleasures of "true" sportsmen. Historian Richard A. Bartlett wrote:

> It is significant that [General William] Strong, who alone caught more trout than the entire party could possibly consume, and killed whole coveys of dusky grouse, and who might well have reflected upon his own gluttony, should have discussed the depletion of game in the park.

It is also significant that the U.S. Army wanted to oust the Interior Department and gain control of the park. This is not surprising from a sportsman's viewpoint. Since long before the American Revolution, officers stationed on the frontier have enjoyed hunting and fishing. In fact, more than a few of these career officers were outright fanatics. Their duties often carried them to far reaches of the continent's virgin wilderness, where fish and game were untapped and where the sport was at its best. It was a chance of a lifetime, and the government paid all expenses, even assigning orderlies to pitch camp and do all the cooking for the officers. Sixty-three-year-old General Marcy was so dedicated he actually endangered his life on this expedition when he fell into the Yellowstone River while fighting a large trout, soaked himself thoroughly, caught a serious fever, but still refused to stop fishing.

We can thank General Strong for keeping very precise statistics on the trip, for much was learned regarding the quality of trout fishing in the Yellowstone River as a result. On August 1, the party was camped near the river, above the upper falls. Strong selected his lightest fly rod and "put on a six-foot leader and three flies—a Gray Professor at the end of the leader and two Brown Hackles above." Strong drifted his traditional wet flies endlessly, but to no avail. Finally he asked his orderly to catch grasshoppers. He attached a fancy new "brilliant fly" (Parmachene Belle?) to the end of his leader along with the live hopper. He placed "three buckshot for sinkers, just above the snell." The eclectic rig did the trick. The following account is in Strong's own words:

> My reel whirled and spun like a buzz-saw, the line went out so fast. I never touched the reel to check the running line til seventy-five feet, at least, was in the water, then I pressed my thumb firmly upon

it and drew gently back the rod . . . I gave him twenty-five or thirty feet more line, then checked again and tried to hold him, but it was no use, the rod bent nearly double, and I had to let him run. My line was one hundred and fifty feet in length, and I knew when it was all out, if the fish still kept in the rapids, I should lose him. . . . Twice in his straight run down the rapid current of the stream he leaped clear from the water, and I saw he was immense—something double or triple the size of any trout I had ever caught. . . . Finally he showed signs of exhaustion; and I managed to get him to the top of the water, and then worked him in close to the shore, where Flynn [the orderly] was waiting to take the line and throw him out, as I had no landing net. . . . He was a fine specimen, and would weigh four pounds if he would weigh an ounce.

By 4:30 P.M. Strong stopped fishing, having hooked 75–100 trout and landed 35. "I never saw a finer string of trout in my life," Strong wrote. "My orderly had strung them on a forked branch of a willow, and the only way we could get the string to camp was by dragging them upon the ground, Flynn taking one side of the branch and I the other." It had been the best day's fishing in William Strong's life.

Other members of the expedition had similar success, and over the next week or so many more trout were caught, some even with flies. At one point in his journal, Strong titillates the antique collectors among us when he reports that he loaned General Forsyth his "light Orvis rod, and although he had great success in striking the fish, it took time and careful management to land them with such light, delicate tackle and in such rapid water." One can't help but speculate which Orvis model was used on that historic trip. Nearly half of the men were fishing with "short, stiff rods," however, and "all had extraordinary luck, so that the pile of trout brought into camp was enormous."

How enormous was it? According to Strong's meticulous statistics, the party was in the park for exactly thirteen days, during which time they caught exactly 3,489 trout, ranging in size from two and a half to four pounds. It doesn't take an expert in mathematics to calculate that these figures translate to over three tons of fish used to feed thirty-five men for two weeks, not to mention a similar "tonnage" of game that was shot. One hundred ten years and two days later I stood in the same stretch of river as General William Strong and enjoyed almost identical success (though I released all of my fish and their average size was slightly smaller than Strong's reported catch). If sports-

men were starting to exploit the Yellowstone in the early 1870s, then how could this quality of fishing have endured here when it was so wantonly destroyed throughout most of the West?

Part of the answer lies in the fact that the Yellowstone country historically was so isolated from large population centers, and part of the answer lies in timely management practices once the river began to degenerate. Before the automobile, the park was almost inaccessible to most middle-class citizens. It did not suffer from market hunting to the extent that other regions of the West suffered (although hunters did take their toll on big game and commercial fishing was legal until 1917). Between 1910 and 1940, less than 100,000 tourists per year visited the park, and only 5 percent of these people fished. From time to time exotics (including bass) were stocked in the river, but none, thankfully, survived. In addition, mining activity did not penetrate the Yellowstone basin as it did in California, Colorado, Montana, and other parts of the West. Although the fishing on accessible waters began deteriorating by the 1920s, it became even worse after World War II. By 1948, the number of tourists visiting the park each year suddenly had skyrocketed to one million. By the 1960s that figure had tripled. The proportion of fishermen was still only 5 percent, but the overall increase still resulted in many more people taking fish from the river. The quality of fishing rapidly decreased during this period.

Some help came in 1953 when the National Park Service stopped stripping cutthroat eggs from six stripping stations on Yellowstone Lake. Since the turn of the century, over eight million eggs had been taken from both the lake and the river, cultured, and the fry returned to Yellowstone waters, but with only poor results. All stocking ceased within the park. The trout were allowed to reproduce naturally, and their numbers increased. During the '50s and '60s research actually discovered that the rapidly increasing angling pressure did not decrease the number of cutthroat in the Yellowstone drainage. What fishing pressure did cause, however, was a decrease in the average size of the fish, as large specimens were creeled faster than juvenile fish could grow to larger sizes. When fishing pressure reached a certain point, the average size of the fish decreased proportionately.

During the '60s bait fishing was banned to promote catch-and-release. By 1971 the five-fish, no-length limit was replaced by a three-fish, fourteen-inch-minimum-length limit. By 1973, the Yellowstone River was a no-kill trout stream. From that point forward, the size of the cutthroats mushroomed. By 1976, the average length of the trout in the river was fifteen inches. By the mid-'80s it was close to seventeen inches and leveling off. The mighty Yellowstone literally had been restored to its former glory in the nick of time. Had its degradation started prior to the 1950s, it is highly likely that lack of scientific knowledge and anti-conservationist attitudes toward curbing bag limits among the pre-war generations would have prevented restoration forever.

Today the quality of angling in the Yellowstone is practically equivalent to what it was during the nineteenth century. The opponents of catch-and-release fishing still criticize the policies that have made it such, however. They contend that mortality among released fish is high, and a two- or three-fish limit should be allowed. A research study conducted by Gresswell, Griffith, and Schill in 1981, however, reported an astounding 3 percent hooking mortality rate among cutthroat trout caught in Yellowstone, a statistic much below the hooking mortality percentages of other catch-and-release waters. The late Charles Brooks of West Yellowstone, Montana, probably knew the river better than any angler. He began fishing it in 1947 when the fish averaged seventeen inches. He saw it decline drastically in the '50s and '60s. Finally, he saw it completely restored before his death in 1986. Writing in *Fishing Yellowstone Waters* (1984), Brooks claimed that in the six miles of open water on the Yellowstone above the falls, it is possible to catch and release "over seventy-five trout averaging two pounds in a day's fishing, and catches of fifty or more are not at all uncommon."

Brooks further asserted that in these six miles the river is "so unbelievably good that it supports about 4500 anglers per mile of stream during the season and still maintains its quality. It is catch-and-release fishing, perhaps the most prolific such piece of water anywhere in the world." I tend to agree with him. Because of its quality, the naturalists and other park personnel regard the Yellowstone River as a natural history museum for the native cutthroat trout. I contend that it is a bit more than this. From an historical perspective too, the Yellowstone is a museum, and its big trout a national treasure. Through enlightened management practices, the Yellowstone River is today an historical exhibit depicting what western anglers witnessed in the age of General William Strong, a living monument to our angling heritage, where you and I can still cast our fly and literally touch the past.

Western Trout Flies:
A Maverick Tradition

It has always struck me as being peculiar that there are so many trout fly variations. When I first got serious about fly-fishing I searched every tackle catalog in existence in an attempt to bring some sort of order out of the madness. Then I read Art Flick's wonderful little book, *A Streamside Guide*. It made a lot of sense. Flick's description of the principal mayfly types, their emergence sequence, their standard dry fly imitations, concisely fit into the great American pattern of reducing and pigeonholing knowledge. My first set of mail-ordered trout flies came in a classy looking box from Orvis. Each specimen was neatly labeled, and the whole collection was appropriately titled "The Art Flick Selection." In the box were the standard Quill Gordons, Hendricksons, Cahills, March Browns, Dun Variants, and the like. The only problem was, I didn't catch too many fish with them, at least not on western streams. The flimsy things got soaked after two drifts, and I spent most of my time false casting, usually in vain.

Only later was I introduced to such flies as the Goofus Bug and Elk Hair Caddis. When I became aware of these so-called "western patterns," my mind boggled. I learned that the Goofus Bug probably imitated a caddis, but not necessarily. Most people referred to it as an "attractor pattern," whatever that meant (aren't all patterns used to "attract" fish?). When I started fishing with nymphs, the confusion became worse. I used Wooly Worms, but was told they were not nymphs. When I asked what they were supposed to imitate, no one knew. I learned that Girdle Bugs only worked in Montana and that I might as well turn them in at the state line when I left. Big, bushy, hair flies, I was told, were necessary for swift western rivers unless mayflies were hatching, in which case I should use an Adams (certainly a contradiction in terms). On the South Platte River, the experts said I should always match the hatch, or "go small," which meant using midges, Blue-winged Olives, Tricos, Blue Duns, and Brassy nymphs in sizes 20–24. I can't even tie a Blue-winged Olive, or for that matter, anything with wings in a size 24. I almost gave up the sport.

Years later, mostly through trial and error rather than from advice, I concluded that the Elk Hair Caddis in various sizes, the Adams, the Goofus Bug, a Joe's Hopper or two, the Royal Wulff, a few stone fly nymphs, Hare's Ear nymphs, Pheasant Tail nymphs, Zug Bugs, and that obscene-looking thing known as a Wooly Bugger, would usually get me results (except on the South Platte) unless, of course, mayfly duns were on the water and exact hatch matching was called for, in which case I could use flies that resembled my old Art Flick selection. When I fished high lakes, a whole different group of flies was put into action. Whew! If you think that's confusing, consider that I have mentioned only a tiny fraction of the patterns designed or adapted to western waters. You will notice too, that some of the flies on that list are eastern and British in origin. Easterners also have a hard time reducing their fly boxes to a few workable patterns, I am sure. But I am convinced that we westerners have it worse. After all, we use many of the eastern varieties in addition to certain patterns specifically developed for the West, which would look foolish drifting down a stream in the Adirondacks. No wonder fly-fishing is called the "thinking man's sport."

One day on the Firehole River I met a jaunty fellow from New York who asked me why there are so many more fly patterns in the West than in the East. I think my reply was accurate. I told him "it's because we have more bugs." Fly-fishing writer John McDonald concurs with this notion in *Quill Gordon*:

> The variety of Western insects has brought about the use of a wider variety of trout flies (including some garish specimens) than is found in the East. From this has come the notion that Western fly-fishing is occupied not only with wild trout but with crude methods.

I don't know about crude methods. Perhaps the fact that the West is not so traditionally wedded to the mayfly accounts for a wider variety of acceptable methods. If so, it has also created some confusion over the profuse number of local patterns tied in this huge geographical area. Certainly the caddis is one of the most, if not *the* most important insect on western waters. But the large stone flies and grasshoppers can get a lot of first-place votes too. The infamous western wind, which can reduce many easterners and their four-weight rods to tears, has made terrestrial insects more important here. In short, the West does have a greater variety of insects of primary important to trout (and fly-fishers) than just the mayfly. As a result of this abundance, tracing the historical development of fly patterns in this huge region is rather like researching the rise and fall of the Roman Empire sans English translations. In many cases, accurate historical records are sketchy at best.

From what records do exist, I finally was able to piece together a somewhat diversified history of several western fly patterns, many of which were invented independently in different regions or borrowed from the East and adapted to western waters. It is commonly accepted among western flytiers that to ascribe origin of certain western flies to only one tier is to offend another who developed the same or similar pattern in a different state or region. But anyway, here goes.

When the big push was made onto the western frontier after the Civil War, most fly-fishers were becoming familiar with the wet fly tradition that was coming into full flower back east. Before the coming of the railroad, western anglers certainly used whatever barnyard fowl or wild birds happened to be handy to fashion their flies. Continuous generic references to "Grey Hackle, Brown Hackle, and Coachmen" flies are abundant in newspaper and periodical reports of the era, indicating that patterns tended to be subdued. This trend may not have been the result of trying to imitate western insects exactly. More likely it was because brightly colored avian resources were simply scarce. Undoubtedly "fancy" Victorian wet fly patterns from the East found their way into the fly books of western anglers after about 1870, but there is surprisingly little mention of them before the last decade of the nineteenth century.

By the early twentieth century, the advances made by Gordon, Steenrod, and others in advancing the "Catskill School" of flytying influenced western anglers when dry fly fishing began to take hold. But this accounts only for mayfly imitation. Almost certainly, new methods (imitation theory, dry fly fishing, etc.) caught on slowly in the isolated West. Eastern tradition was based on the English model,

which centered around the mayfly. In the West other insects were more important sources of trout food, and thus western needs were more varied. It was not until well into the twentieth century that a distinctive western style of flytying emerged – at least few records exist before that time. Due perhaps to geographical isolation or regional provincialism, innovative western flytiers simply did not become known to us much before the 1920s.

One of the earliest definitive accounts is that of a Missoula, Montana, angler by the name of Norman Means who developed a series of early cork-bodied stone fly imitations he dubbed "Bunyon Bugs" around 1927. About the same time, another Missoula tier, Franz Pott, pioneered the technique of weaving hair-bodied flies – a technique refined and even attributed later to Dan Bailey of West Yellowstone. By the 1930s, Californian Don Martinez started developing caddis imitations, but he is best remembered for the Wooly Worm, a palmer-hackled wet fly that looks much like the British Zulu. Dan Bailey, a New Yorker who settled in West Yellowstone, not only refined woven-body nymph techniques but also expanded the popular Wulff flies for western waters after the '30s. Al Troth of Dillon, Montana, developed numerous western fly patterns, as did "Polly" Roseborough, Peter Schwab, and others by the middle decades of the twentieth century.

In all likelihood the technique of fishing and tying weighted nymphs had numerous independent origins throughout the U.S. As early as the 1860s fly-fishers would pinch on a piece of buckshot to get their flies down to the bottom. But in Colorado, Cliff Welch is credited, by at least one source, with advancing this commonly used technique for fly-fishers stalking the wary South Platte trout. Welch, a member of the prestigious Wigwam Fly Fishing Club, was fishing the river near Deckers with much success one fine August day in 1935. In fact, so the story goes, Welch was setting the hook in one big rainbow right after another while his companions couldn't buy a strike. When asked what he was using, Welch produced a size 12 March Brown nymph tied to the end of a nine-foot tapered leader with a split shot attached about a foot above the fly. Club officials were furious. They demanded that Welch give up the practice or be censured from the Wigwam Club, since using weight was not considered proper fly-fishing. Welch discontinued the use of the lead (at least on the club's private fishing grounds), but the famous South

Platte weighted-nymphing technique caught on and has become a common feature of the sport today. Since the '30s there have been many fly-fishers developing new techniques and inventing distinctive flies to match western insects, but these developments did not become widely known until after the frontier had long passed. Before then, most flies, especially early caddis imitations, were local specialties that did not become so widespread as to receive much press, or simply came from eastern tradition and eastern tackle shops.

Earlier innovators, and certainly there were some, were simply too isolated geographically to become noticed on the national scene, and their contributions were thus mostly lost. Even in later years it is sometimes hard to determine exactly who developed any particular fly. For example the Goofus Bug, as it is known in Wyoming, or Humpy, as it is known in Colorado, is credited by a few people to Pat Barnes of West Yellowstone. Many more agree, however, that Jack Horner invented the fly. Still others claim that it had several independent origins. Some western tiers simply adapted eastern patterns to meet their needs. The Mizzoulian Spook is a good example. It is really a white-mottled Minnow type of pattern, which some say is just a western version of Gordon's old Bumblepuppy developed for the Catskills. Many small, delicate mayfly patterns including the Quill Gordon itself are readily used or adapted to western size requirements, and it can be argued that a size 18 Adams may be the most popular all-around dry fly in the West. In any case, the West is still the largest section of the country, and relatively obscure variations of fly patterns both old and new still proliferate regionally.

I rather like to think that this proliferation reflects the basic human nature of the region. I suppose western flies are kind of like western fishing guides. Take for example the young man who once guided me on the Madison River. A life-long resident of Montana, the handsome youth appeared every inch a cowboy. We rattled down the highway toward the river in his souped-up Chevy pickup with the inevitable Stetson hat hung over the rearview mirror and the inevitable lever action Winchester hung ominously in the rear window. The truck had an audio tape deck, and just when I thought I had the guy stereotyped as the Willie Nelson or Hank Williams, Jr., type, he pulled out a box of cassette tapes containing the complete works of Wolfgang Amadeus Mozart, inserted *Don Giovanni*, act 2, and turned up the volume full blast. All the way to the river we were edified by the

Vienna Symphony Orchestra. Trout flies found in the vest boxes of western fly-fishers are much like modern westerners themselves – they simply refuse to be stereotyped, standardized, categorized, and pigeonholed. Their fly selections are in fact eclectic and cosmopolitan; in a word – maverick.

If sorting out regional fly patterns is confusing, so is determining which insect hatch fly-fishers most like to match. It seems that every western angler has his or her preference. While most easterners agree that the mayfly is tops, westerners have, once again, a wider variety to choose from for first-class sport. Many prefer to match the hatches of tiny midges on 7X tippets on the fabled Harriman Park section of the Henry's Fork of the Snake. Others feel the giant stone fly hatch of *Pteronarcys californica*, the so-called salmonfly hatch, cannot be equaled. Who can forget Charles Brooks's description in *Fishing Yellowstone Waters* of meeting the "head of the hatch" on the Madison River? After tying into forty good trout within two feet or so of the streambanks, his old Pflueger Medalist reel literally "screamed and chattered and clattered and rattled and fell apart" as the frame screws became so overworked that they fell out, leaving Charlie standing there with the separated reel spool in his hand and a five-pound trout on the end of 150 feet of line and an 0X leader. Then there are those who favor the seemingly ever-present caddis hatches. The famous "Mother's Day hatch" on the Madison can fill the air with so many caddis that the angler has the impression he is in the midst of a winter blizzard.

For others, however, there is simply no greater sport in the world than fishing grasshopper imitations. The audible "plop" of the big fly cast to a secret pool beneath a grassy bank, the violent splashing, slashing strike of a big brown in a meadow stream may simply be the height of the fly-fishing sport. And for the most part, it is typically western. Stone flies and caddis are closely associated with western fly-fishing, it's true. But for many, myself included, August and September are the finest months of the year, for that's when the hoppers come out. As John McDonald said, "Farther west, fly-fishermen discovered the grasshopper, and not being traditionalists at the expense of good fishing, they made or adopted a basic new fly."

Brother, did they! Throughout most of the West, the grasshopper is the one terrestrial insect imitated (considering the wide array of local patterns) almost as profusely as aquatic bugs. Furthermore, the hopper has a long tradition in the lore, angling and otherwise, of the western frontier—much more so than either the mayfly or the caddis. Throughout the literature of fly-fishing the early West, the attributes of *Orthoptera* are frequently mentioned. In fact, the grasshopper might just be the most infamous insect of all in the history of the West. The annals of the Great Plains are filled with reports of prairie farmers being wiped out by the insects. Great plagues of the pests (many were actually Rocky Mountain locusts) would move by the billions in great clouds all the way from Texas to the Dakotas. They could devastate a grain field in a few hours' time. In 1874, a three-foot drift of the insects actually halted a Union Pacific train near Kearney, Nebraska. Even today, grasshopper infestations are common.

The hopper fly was not originally a western or even American innovation. As early as 1676 Charles Cotton described a dressing for a "Green Grasshopper" with a "dubbing of green and yellow wool mixed, ribbed over with green silk, and a red capon's feather over all." But, as A. Courtney Williams admitted in *A Dictionary of Trout Flies*, hopper flies and fishing "have never made much appeal to English fly-fishermen." In the eastern U.S., Orvis and Cheney illustrated a grasshopper pattern, trout fly number 56 to be exact, on one of the colorful plates in their classic *Fishing with the Fly* (1886), although the typically colorful Victorian "fancy" pattern certainly resembles nothing I've ever observed hopping around in my garden.

Later, the Letort Hopper, made from deer hair, was developed by Ernest Schwiebert for use on Pennsylvania streams. But in the Midwest and West the hopper came into its glory. The Michigan Hopper Fly, later called Joe's Hopper, became the standard pattern. Today there are many local variations of the innocuous insect, some so realistic that they fool many anglers. In fact, it can be argued that the hopper imitation in general is the most distinct trout fly identified with the West today, although caddis imitations are probably actually fished more extensively throughout much of the season.

During the nineteenth century, on the frontiers of the West, when Victorian hopper patterns were not available, local patterns scarce or nonexistent, and August rises prolific, many anglers, including more than a few purists, were not above using the real McCoy on the ends of their gut leaders. Consider the success of the W.E. Strong party, from a previous chapter, using live specimens on the Yellowstone River in 1875.

stealthfully dropping their bait into the eddies made by the rapid current, and then yanking the wary trout out of the water without a second's delay, the mystery was fully explained."

Vest told the president that the soldiers were using live grasshoppers. From that point forward, the president's luck improved dramatically. No photographic record exists of President Arthur in the act

In at least one instance hopper fishing (live or otherwise) involved an American president. In 1883, the completion of the Northern Pacific Railroad had suddenly made Yellowstone National Park relatively accessible to a host of market hunters who were exploiting the big game of the region. At the urging of General Phillip Sheridan, Senator George G. Vest of Missouri, and *Forest and Stream* editor George Bird Grinnell, a party of dignitaries set out to tour the region, ostensibly to garner support for protecting the park from private enterprise, but in reality to capitalize on a good excuse for a fishing vacation. The party of ten, supported by a seventy-five-man escort of the Fifth Cavalry, left Chicago for Rawlins, Wyoming, by train on August 1, 1883. The party included President Chester A. Arthur, an ardent fly-fisher who never wanted the office he held (as vice-president he had assumed the presidency after the assassination of James Garfield). During the previous winter, Arthur had ordered fifty dollars worth of tackle especially for the trip.

From Rawlins, the party journeyed the remaining 350 miles on horseback. The rotund Arthur, every bit the Victorian gentleman despite his obesity, must have looked amusing on the last leg of the trip. To date no chief executive had ever visited the national park. General Sheridan planned the trip, and the agenda called for the party to camp on a trout stream every night. On August 8, the party camped on the Bull Fork of Wyoming's Wind River. According to a reporter, "The President" proved to be a "good horseman and came into camp like an old campaigner." That evening the president took his first string of trout on a fly from western waters. The reporter did not reveal what fly he used.

A few days later, on the Gros Ventre River, however, the president's luck seemed to diminish. Senator Vest, who was also an experienced angler, later wrote that President Arthur's "array of tackle was enough to bewilder an entire fishing club." An old private photograph I once saw showed Arthur's catch of cutthroats from the Gros Ventre. Next to the nice string of about twenty fish was a fine rod that looked very much like an early Leonard. Despite their abilities, though, the president and Senator Vest could not seem to match the catches brought in by the cavalrymen and mule drivers. On the morning of August 12, therefore, Senator Vest decided to do some spying. Observing the other successful anglers, Vest noted that "when I saw the caution with which they crawled around the rocks and bushes, of fishing on this trip. Neither do we have a record of what specific flies he used. Perhaps some colorful Victorian hopper imitations were in the president's vest and were indeed utilized, but most probably Arthur made do with the real thing, as W.E. Strong had done eight years before. Nevertheless, the president became skilled at dunking a grasshopper and an enthusiastic advocate of the technique, judging from his success on the trip after August 12. We can visualize him sneaking up on the stream on his hands and knees and gently plopping a fat hopper along the bank. One would at least like to believe that the president sought out grasshopper imitations from the great eastern tackle houses after his return to Washington. Hopper fishing certainly could have made him aware of exact imitation theory in a hurry.

Eventually, the party went on to fish the Yellowstone River and Yellowstone Lake as well. The trip brought attention to Arthur and favorable publicity for protecting the park. Denver journalist Eugene Field even amused his readers with jocular stories of President Arthur beating Shoshone Indians at poker and causing one chief to vow that he would move farther west in order to escape Great White Fathers who spoiled the local fishing. In later decades many other national dignitaries would sample the great hopper fishing of the West. Most of them would use standardized hopper flies like the Joe's Hopper, or perhaps even a few locally developed patterns.

Although the tradition of western fly development might be more obscured than that of the East and Great Britain, especially when it comes to imitating terrestrial insects, whenever I cast a Joe's Hopper to a far bank on a windy August day, I am always reminded of the historical link I have with the twenty-first president of the U.S. After all, I'm using a pattern typically associated with the West—a real maverick from purist tradition perhaps, but if Chester A. Arthur had lived to see its widespread development, one that would surely possess official presidential sanction.

The Gilded Age in California:
An Image of the Western Fly-Fisher

Since I became fascinated with the rich and colorful heritage of sporting tradition I have always held in my mind a stereotype of what the typical Victorian fly-fisher looked like. Undoubtedly the proper eastern gentleman who would frequent the trout streams of New England or New York had a big "walrus" moustache and perhaps a full beard. He might wear a vest and a white shirt with detachable starched collar. A wide, patterned necktie was always appropriate. His coat might have been fashioned from rugged yellow canvas, but more commonly it was of grey or brown tweed—lapelled of course. Tweed knickers complemented the rest of his attire along with black wool stockings. By the end of the nineteenth century, black rubber hip boots were used extensively, but in earlier years knee-high "rubbers," the kind Atlantic salmon-fishing guides in Iceland still wear, were most appropriate. Add to this a penchant for sporty tweed caps in Brighton, Windsor, or Polo shape, depending on the year in question, and you have the smart figure of a typical late-nineteenth-century eastern fly-fisher.

For women fly-fishers (and contrary to popular belief, there were some) full skirts were frequently worn along with fashionable wide-brimmed straw bonnets and hats complete with gossamer veils to protect the lady's face and neck from mosquitoes and black flies. Of course she would always be held gently by the arm and escorted into the water by a courtly gentleman until she had reached a reasonable casting position (who wouldn't need help wearing a get-up like that in a swiftly moving stream?).

High fashion in personal attire was not the only "statement" affluent eastern fly-fishers made. In habits of behavior as well these sportsmen helped shape the image of fly-fishing as a stylish recreation. After the Civil War, when the once-dramatic fishing grounds of Long Island and urban New England were finally depleted, these sports boarded ornate passenger cars of the proliferating railroads for outings in the Adirondacks. Fashionable spas and hotels that catered to the pretentious tastes of stylish Bostonians and New Yorkers sprang up along the streams and lakes of these mountains. In many cases the elegant Victorian hotel buildings of New York State's lake region matched the fancy trout flies used by their patrons for ostentation and gaudiness. Certainly there were many modest fly-fishers in the East at this time, but it is the image of these Adirondack dandies fishing for a few hours during the day and then wining and dining for many more hours during the evening that has contributed significantly to the stereotype of the fly-fisher as snob—a designation that is still (unfortunately) associated with the sport to some degree.

When the Rangeley Lakes region of Maine was penetrated in the 1870s, anglers bent on catching the huge brook trout and landlocked salmon inhabiting those waters found the fishing lodges more primitive in that comparatively isolated area but no less convivial. For throughout the East, fly-fishing was a convivial sport. Whether headquartered in elegant Adirondack hotel suites or crowded into a rustic log cabin in the north woods of Maine, exclusive angling clubs purchased large tracts of land for their private sport. Before we condemn these new industrial order nobles as prime examples of late-nineteenth-century laissez faire, Republican voting, Social Darwinistic monopolizers, we must remember that it was chiefly through their conservation efforts that any viable eastern trout fisheries survived the nineteenth century at all.

Besides, these eastern anglers were only imitating their British cousins. Judging from the themes of popular angling writers of the early nineteenth century, eastern sportsmen had begun this mimicry in earnest about ten years or so before the Civil War. One of the truly great sporting journalists in the U.S. during this era was a man by the name of Henry William Herbert, known affectionately to his readers by the nom de plume of Frank Forester. According to Forester and his successors in the press, and as depicted by such contemporary painters as Arthur F. Tait, affluent sportsmen in New York's "lakes," whether spending a month at a grandiose hotel or a humble shanty, supplied themselves lavishly with "rare cheeses, spiced beef, cigars, whiskey, claret, and grandly wrought [fly] rods." The provisions of the camp, argued Forester, reflected an awakening consciousness among Americans of the British tradition of elegance in all matters pertaining to the sport. Of course the technique of fishing "fancy" wet flies became refined and even became associated with the U.S. But in viewing fishing as a social sport, in the preemption and conservation of fishing grounds and even in manners, mores, and dress, the eastern fly-fisher imitated the British fly-fisher during the Gilded Age. He wanted to go in style.

When trying to envision the figure of the typical western fly-fisher of the nineteenth century, the task is not quite so easy. The idea persists, perhaps in a pejorative way, that the elegant costume of conservative coat and knickers was forever altered with the California gold rush when a small-time Jewish peddler bought up surplus sail cloth from abandoned ships in San Francisco Harbour, fashioned it into rugged pants, and changed the way westerners (and perhaps the world) dressed from that time forward. And if you are the type who likes to devalue the contribution of the 1853 Levi Strauss patent toward the development of a distinctly American fashion consciousness, consider that none other than Ralph Lauren resides in Colorado and wears Levis all the time. They are the best thing I have ever found for trout fishing–beats a tie and tweed coat every time. In addition, the stereotype of the western fly-fisher of the nineteenth century, if one exists at all, is that as a true individualist, he usually fished the remote and dangerous wilderness alone or with only a few brave and hearty companions. The tweed would give way to Levis, and the claret from the family cellar would be replaced with a pint bottle of cheap bourbon purchased in a seedy clapboard saloon.

To a significant degree this stereotype of the rugged frontier individualist has continued to inflate westerners' egos down to the present day. To some, the mythic hero of the West is still the loner– the borderline-violent, independent maverick. This John Wayne role model has even affected the way many westerners have responded to the environment. There are those who view the public land as belonging to everybody, and therefore as nobody's responsibility, and there are those who believe passionately that we are all responsible for its complete preservation. This is the basic uncompromising mentality of many modern westerners. Today, states historian Wallace Stegner, "the battlegrounds of the environmental movement lie in the Western public lands," chiefly due to the folk hero myth (and its various interpretations) of the individualistic western outdoorsman.

Certainly it can be argued that individualism had a lot to do with settling the frontier and making the U.S. great. But it is also true that the theme of individualism has been overplayed–especially when we try to stereotype the appearance and habits of western sportsmen. Among westerners of the late nineteenth century, the first and primary goal, after staking a claim or clearing the land, was simply to make money so that eastern "culture" and "civilization" could be reproduced in the new land. Once that goal had been accomplished, westerners acted a lot like easterners, even when it came to such comparatively unimportant pursuits as fly-fishing. The tastes of affluent Victorians in the West's few metropolises of the nineteenth century, principally San Francisco and Denver, could be strikingly similar to the tastes of the elite back east.

Both cities were made wealthy by a new American crop of super millionaires who amassed their fortunes, in one way or another, because of the presence of gold and silver. From their estates on Telegraph Hill or Capitol Hill, they frequently left for the wilderness on extended fishing expeditions complete with servants, cigars, claret, and fine imported liquor. The West had its dandies too.

These more affluent westerners imitated in both dress and habit the supposedly more conservative eastern fly-fisher, just as the eastern sportsman imitated his British cousin. What may come as a real surprise is that many urban middle-class westerners did the same whenever they could. Both photographs and angling literature of the era support this contention. Consider the following story from one of the truly great fly-fishing books of the last century, which not only reveals the general appearance of a group of western anglers but their habits as well.

One of the true collector's items among Victorian fishing books is the volume by Orvis and Cheney entitled *Fishing with the Fly*, published in 1886. The book contains twenty-four contemporary fishing stories contributed by serious anglers of the era. Most of the stories deal with such great nineteenth-century eastern fishing grounds as Maine's Rangeley Lakes and Ontario's big brook trout country along the Nipigon River. One story, however, is quite different. It relates the adventures of a group of middle-class San Franciscans on a two-week camping trip to the Merced River in California's Yosemite Valley circa 1880. No railroad penetrated the Yosemite Valley, so the entourage traveled part of the way by prairie schooner, but in every other way, and like their eastern counterparts of the Gilded Age, this group went in style. Surely the story has aroused the curiosity of generations of Americans who have believed that individualistic westerners usually fished alone from crude wilderness camps.

This party of San Francisco dandies was seven in number, and from the author's description, they made quite a sight. There was a rather rotund "Judge" and his even more rotund wife (the "Judgess"), who, if she was termed "fat and forty," the description would "fall far short of the truth." The couple came to the Sierras for the same reasons their eastern brethern went to the Adirondacks—they were on the "verge of decline and sought recuperation in the forest." This unlikely pair was chaperoning a very fashion-conscious young woman whose name was Madge. Madge was referred to by the bachelors of San

Francisco as a "rattler" because of her incessant flirting. Accordingly, Madge flirted with every man in sight during the trip, including "stray herdsmen" on the journey to the mountains, an "English baronet at a Yosemite hotel," and when nothing else was available, the Judge and a mild-mannered clergyman ("his Reverence"), the fourth member of the expedition.

Madge's conservatively attired brother, identified only as "the Doctor," was along to sketch and paint the valley with his water colors. From all evidence, the Doctor was matched only by the Judge for his arrogant behavior and pomposity. A heroic type named Jack was the sixth member of the group. Young and virile, Jack was thoroughly dedicated to fly-fishing. The last member of the party was Ah Yang, a Chinese servant who was brought along to wash and cook and generally wait on the others hand and foot. Yang cursed a lot throughout the story, argued with the pompous Judge, and insulted the arrogant Doctor. Obviously very independent, Yang's behavior goes a long way in dispelling the myth of the obsequious Chinese coolie of the nineteenth-century West. This rather comical group comprised typically Victorian, urban, middle-class individuals who might be taking an outing anywhere in the nation. They would not have been out of place in the Adirondacks.

Jack, of course, was the hero of the story, and like all heroes he was faced with a series of problems to overcome. Aside from losing several nights' sleep spent gallantly helping the porcine Judgess back into the hammock she repeatedly fell out of, Jack found his major antagonist to be the Doctor. After setting up an elaborate camp, Jack finally uncased his rod and produced his "long-cherished fly book." Many of the controversies and prejudices that exist among anglers today were also present in the 1880s. After scowling languidly at Jack's treasures, the Doctor turned up his nose at the flies and snorted.

"Pooh!" he said. "I hope you don't expect to catch any trout with those things in Yosemite! Everybody knows that the Merced trout don't take the fly." He went on to say that, "with a common string, such as any grocer would use to tie up a package of tea, a good strong hook, and a worm," he would catch in the same time "more fish than could all the sportsmen of California, fishing with fancy flies." To prove his point the Doctor marched off in the direction of majestic El Capitan with a cane pole and a can of worms. By evening he returned to camp, wet and hungry, and in a "sulphurous mood, but

with four unmistakable [rainbow] trout" for breakfast. For the next day or so Jack sat on his bunk and brooded as the teasing Madge sought his attentions. Eventually, the remainder of the party ventured off to ascend Clouds' Rest and tour the base of Yosemite Falls.

With their departure Jack mustered the courage to rig his flies and defiantly head toward nearby Mirror Lake. His only companion was the boisterous Ah Yang. Nervously, Jack cast his flies far out beneath the shadows of some willow bushes along the shore. He made two more casts. Then the first rainbow rose and struck with a fury. Yang was ready with the landing net, and after a short struggle, the fish was landed. As the sport continued, Jack relaxed a bit, but Yang's

excitement grew more intense. Soon the action was furious. Yang was jumping with glee. "Fifty-sleven [sic], Jack. Hi! that big fish; fifty-eight . . . Hold him tight, 'Rusalem . . . Pull like hella, fifty-nine!"

At last the long shadows under the massive mountain domes deepened into twilight, and the river became shrouded in mist. Triumphantly, Jack returned to camp where he turned into the Judgess's hammock with a smirk while Yang went down the valley and registered at the hotel for a chance to sleep in a real bed. That night Jack slept soundly for the first time in many days—and no doubt dreamed of big native rainbow trout.

The following evening, when the balance of the party returned to camp from their excursion, Jack and Yang had prepared a feast that rivaled any repast ever served al fresco in the mountains of California (or for that matter, New York). The dinner "began, continued, and ended with fish" cooked in every imaginable way Ah Yang knew. There were starched linen napkins, sterling silver forks, and vintage wine procured from the hotel in the valley as well as "all sorts of [exotic] garnitures of Yang's contrivance. Madge was in ecstacies, and even the Judgess expressed approval." Everyone had a good time—except the Doctor. After the meal the party heard the details of the catch. But the Doctor frowned disapprovingly. Finally he blatantly accused Jack of procuring the fish from local anglers after bribing Yang to hold his tongue.

"You think you heap smart," Yang barked at the Doctor. "Jack heap sabee how [to] fish, and you *no* sabee, but me sabee *you*. Last Fliday you go fish, and when me water horse, see Injin sellee you fish. I sabee *you*." In the rollicking laughter that followed the Doctor blustered away toward his blankets muttering curses at Yang and the others. His worm fishing foray, it seemed, had been nothing but a sham.

The party lingered another week in the Yosemite Valley. Madge and the reverend became "quite expert with the fly." The Merced River supplied the entourage with fish every day. "Many strings of trout were sent to fellow-campers" and to guests at the hotel. One "little hamper made the long journey by stage and rail to San Francisco." The "trout-camp," as it was called, became legendary in the valley; photographs of the catch even appeared on the pages of the *Stockton Independent* and the *Sacramento Bee*. Jack had accomplished his purpose. He had not come to Yosemite in vain, exclaiming later that he had never experienced "such keen enjoyment with the fly as on that afternoon at Mirror Lake."

As a graduate student I would often make the long drive up from Palo Alto, California, through foothills thick with manzanita and live oak, to fish the streams and high lakes of Yosemite—John Muir's "Range of Light." Inevitably, I would think of that delightful little story told so long ago in Orvis and Cheney's classic. At the time I first started fishing Yosemite, the backpacking craze of the late 1960s and early 1970s was really catching on. Long-haired young men and women literally overflowed the trails to the national park's high lakes and stream meadows. Many of them carried fishing rods lashed to their backpacks. I have packed literally hundreds of miles in search of elusive trout waters deep in the fastness of wilderness mountains. From Montana to New Mexico I have experienced unequaled sport far from the nearest road.

I suppose that to many, the backpacking fisherman, trudging up the switchbacks of some far-off trail attired in twill shorts and a khaki shirt, conceivably might be the stereotype of the modern western fly-fisher. To others, the long pack trains of horses or mules, and in recent years, llamas, led by a tanned and leathery faced wrangler-guide wearing a sweat-stained Stetson and faded Levis fulfills the quintessential image of fly-fishing the West. But whenever I make the journey to fish Yosemite, it seems I always reverse my usual patterns of appearance and behavior. After all, a complete change of pace now and then, unrestricted by stereotypes, is what being a "maverick westerner" is really all about. So, I register at one of the historic old hostelries in the region. I order a glass of claret in the ornate saloon. I sleep on a real feather bed. I might even sport a tweed cap (a coat and tie is just asking too much) while casting a Victorian-era Royal Coachman wet fly in the crystal green waters of the Merced. For every so often, you see, like my ancestors, in both the East and the West, I like to go in style.

A Rod Maker for the West

I suppose it's true with any hobby, that once we become hopelessly afflicted, we start to collect every piece of paraphernalia we can get our hands on that even remotely pertains to our interests. As I'm sure you are aware, fly-fishing is no exception. If you are anything like me, you went through a phase where you simply had to have every new gadget on the market. At one time my vest was filled to capacity with fly threaders, tippet gauges, knot tiers, plastic-coated hatch charts for every stream in North America, and the like. I never used most of it, and after several years of carrying the junk around, I finally relegated what I now refer to as the "stuff," to a dark corner in my tackle bag in hopes that the passage of a few years would elevate some of it to the status of valuable collector items (so far, no such luck).

After we realize that it's no fun wading through a stream carrying double our weight in "stuff," do we stop? No! Instead we trim down the vest and then start to collect more desirable (and expensive) items. The most hopeless among us find our wallets wearing thin when the antique bug hits us with full force. Bamboo fly rods and vintage reels are the more popular antique items for collectors. I've never been a big collector of antique bamboo, thank heavens. I'm just too destructive. It's not that I haven't learned to handle hang-ups in the stream. I just have a bad habit of falling down on slippery rocks. Invariably I find myself sitting on my good fly rods (and, yes, I do use wading cleats). One particular Orvis Battenkill (which is too light to use anyway, except on small streams that seem to have an abundance of algae on the bottom) has simply had too many blanks replaced for me to consider fishing with expensive bamboo (not to mention expensive "antique" bamboo) very frequently, and I can't imagine buying one to hang on the wall or shove into a closet.

Consequently, I collect old reels, mostly Hardys and Orvises. It's harder to do any real damage that way, although there have been a few exceptions even for the strongest of my reels. I do enjoy the tradition surrounding old bamboo rods, however, and I love to read the accounts of how these rods were made and who made them. Almost everyone is familiar with the Garrisons, Paynes, Thomases, Leonards, Gillums, and Orvises. The "top of the line" eastern split-bamboos were the state of the rod maker's art and served generations of affluent fly-fishers. After Hiram Leonard refined the milling process to more easily produce fine fly rods in his Catskill factory during the post-Civil War era, the bamboo rod business really took off. In fact, the Victorian fly-fisher had more manufacturers to choose from than does the modern-day angler.

Of course, some of these eastern gems found their way West before 1900 via the mail-order catalog and the transcontinental railroad, or in the possession of vacationing anglers. Consider the Orvis rod with the W.E. Strong party in Yellowstone in 1875. Also consider how light that rod was. Strong commented on several occasions that the willowy little Orvis just couldn't handle the big Yellowstone cutthroats. We don't know for sure if that rod was bamboo, but it was definitely designed for eastern streams. Back in 1875 fly-fishers were beginning to realize that fishing conditions in the West might require heavier and stronger equipment than what was commonly manufactured for principally eastern markets. Because the East had a much greater population than did the West, westerners were pretty much left to their own devices to meet their unique angling needs in the early years. One option was to custom-order a rod from the East. About 1879, Hiram Leonard custom-built a rod for the Earl of Dunraven. The six-strip calcutta bamboo fly rod was 11-feet-4-inches long, triple jointed, and weighed 8-1/4 ounces. Complete with German silver ferrules and English-style cork grip and reel seat, this rod just might have been the first produced by a major manufacturer for the express purpose of fishing western waters. Unfortunately, no important western rod manufacturer yet existed, and it would be a long while before any rod manufacturer would find a profitable market in the trans-Missouri region. Nothing much happened until about the 1920s.

By that decade long-distance casting tournaments were quite fash-

ionable among angling clubs across the nation. A few western rod-
builder hobbyists began constructing sticks that would soon set new
distance casting world records. Perhaps these new world records were
more an effect than a cause, however, because western anglers primarily
demanded stiff, strong-backboned rods that would perform well in
stiff wind on big rivers, while at the same time delicately cast a dry
fly to selective trout. Undoubtedly, one of the most important fly
rod manufacturers in the West at this time was Edwin Courtney Powell
of Maysville, California. Beginning with his first catalog dated March
20, 1919, Powell began producing rods that were nothing short of
revolutionary. His laminated, semi-hollow, split-bamboo rod, famous
U.S. Patent #1,932,986, set a high standard for western fly rods during
the 1930s. The outer bamboo fibers of the blanks were actually glued

to a wood interior and then hollowed out. The result was a light but extremely strong and flexible fly rod. You will pay a premium price for a classic Powell bamboo fly rod today.

In 1947, Edwin Courtney Powell's son Walton went into business on his own, first in Belmont and later in Chico, California. Today, his famous "Signature" and "Golden Signature" rods are the state of the art among western bamboo fly rods. In 1927 Lew Stoner and Robert Winther began one of the finest rod manufacturing companies in the West. Sometime during the late 1930s they adopted the name "R.L. Winston." The R.L. Winston company employed a rod maker by the name of Doug Merrick who became something of a legend in his own time and went on to give the firm an international reputation for high quality. In 1974, Tom Morgan purchased the firm, along with Merrick, and eventually moved it to the edge of the Rockies, in Twin Bridges, Montana, where R.L. Winston continues to make some of the finest rods in the West. Their "pullman green" graphite models are superb, and the choice of many a western angler, myself included.

There were other western manufacturers of fine bamboo fly rods. The Weir family, E.G. Howells, Goodwin Granger, and others all turned out wonderful products. Most of them are from the West Coast, and their really strong rods were designed, of course, for salmon and steelhead. These were the rods that set new casting distance records. The fine craftsmanship and subsequent prestige that was accrued by these firms meant that their products were not inexpensive. Your basic middle-class fly-fisher who had to work for a living just couldn't afford to own very many of these fine fly rods. Throughout my research into rod history, I have continually kept an eye out for an outstanding rod maker who was, perhaps, more typical of the type of middle-class individuals who originally won the West. I wanted a regular guy who came west to seek his calling and found it not serving the elite but by providing a vastly superior service or product for the great bulk of the middle class.

Ever since I was a boy I had heard of the renowned Wright & McGill Company of Denver. Their giant factory on the plains has literally supplied the nation with reasonably priced rods for many years. But somehow their giant corporate image didn't strike me as being quite the "pioneer" operation I was seeking. To my complete surprise, I found the guy I was looking for right under my nose, in Denver,

Colorado. I was glad my "fly rod pioneer" was not from the West Coast like all the rest. During the same time that the "big boys" were supplying the wealthier fly-fishers of the West with superior but expensive fly rods, a Swedish immigrant to Colorado by the name of William "Bill" Phillipson was turning out what I feel were the best all-around bamboo fly rods for a reasonable price ever manufactured for western trout fishing.

Phillipson had a spirit of independence akin to the pioneer merchants and manufacturers who first settled the urban frontiers of the Old West. Born in Sweden on December 4, 1904, Phillipson migrated to the U.S. at age eighteen and went to work for the Granger Rod Company in Denver in 1925. Recognized as a fine craftsman, Phillipson rose to the head of production in the company upon Granger's death in 1931. Anticipating a post-war economic boom, including an increased demand for fine bamboo fly rods, Phillipson went into business for himself beginning in 1946. The firm was never very big. At the height of bamboo rod production, the Phillipson Rod Company only turned out between 8000 and 10,000 rods annually. But what rods they were.

Phillipson himself designed and perfected a new type of machine for cutting bamboo strips. The machine turned out six strips per minute with little, if any, loss of precision. Perhaps his greatest achievement came as a result of his pioneering experiments with the impregnation process. Impregnation of bamboo rods with resin was being attempted by a number of rod makers in the country by the 1950s and is most closely associated with the achievements of Wes Jordan at the Orvis Company. Phillipson rods were soaked in resin only after the six bamboo strips had been glued up into a rod blank. Consequently, the resin did not penetrate into the pithy interior of the blank. The result was a moisture-proofed rod of extreme durability, yet light enough in weight to still maintain the equivalent line weights of a similar-sized nonimpregnated fly rod.

Fittings, as well, were improved. Phillipson's nickel silver ferrules were tapered down to a very thin but strong edge (when new) so that they actually would flex with the rod rather than create resistance. The rich, walnut-colored fly rods were beautiful when fitted out with their black-and-white jasper windings. A friend of mine once let me cast his 1950s vintage Phillipson rod on the South Platte River. The six-weight stick had amazing power for its size and yet dropped a delicate #20 Blue-winged Olive on the quiet pools without so much as a dimple. I've cast a lot of bamboo rods (when their owners will let me), and it is my opinion that Phillipsons were the best all-around bamboo fly rods ever made for typical western fishing. Sure the Powells and Winstons are great, perhaps slightly better. But they were, and still are, more expensive. That was the factor that made Phillipsons so wonderful.

The "Paragon" model sold for about $19.95 in the 1950s. The top of the line model was the "Premium," which sold for $75. In between was the "Paramount" at around $50. The "Powr Pakt" sold for $37.50 if you could find it in your heart to excuse the spelling of its name, and the "Pacemaker" went for $25. The Pacemaker must have kept the hearts of a lot of anglers beating fast as they cast their flies to big South Platte trout, for it was the most popular model and perhaps the highest quality rod on the market for the price.

Bill Phillipson added glass rods to his line in 1951, which boosted his total production to between 25,000 and 30,000 rods annually. In 1972, Phillipson sold his company to the 3M Corporation and remained an advisor to the company. But for the most part after that date, Bill Phillipson went fishing. His rod making abilities were only equaled by his flycasting skills. In a tournament at Altmont, Colorado, in 1934, Phillipson had set a new world flycasting distance record of 140 feet. Up until a few years ago he could be seen frequently prowling the banks of the South Platte with a Stetson on his head and his glasses reflecting the sunlight. He could strike one big rainbow after another while the rest of us only got a lot of exercise flexing our casting arms. On November 14, 1987, Bill Phillipson died of Alzheimer's disease in Denver, at the age of eighty-two. The fly-fishing fraternity will sorely miss him. Here was a man who insisted on quality and opportunity not only for the elite, but for the masses as well, a quality that possesses the very spirit and intention of the old pioneer dream of western individualism.

So I guess, clumsiness aside, I will have to keep my eyes open for an old Phillipson rod. And the real beauty of them is that they *can* be found for about the price of a new graphite fly rod. Bill Phillipson's intentions, it seems, are still alive and well. I'll look for one of the older models that is not impregnated. The ferrules wore a lot better on those rods—and that's important for a klutz like me. But I promise you that if I do come to own one of these western classics someday, I will hold it out at arm's length while wading over slippery rocks.

The Gentle Art:
Woman's Place Is on the Stream

It was one of those pewter gray mountain evenings, melancholy yet sanguine. A chilling fog hung over the Madison Valley. It penetrated my wool buffalo plaid shirt and soaked through my skin to the very core of my body. I felt as if the cold had originated inside the marrow of my bones and was now radiating outward in a frantic effort to escape, leaving its host weak and drained in the process. Instinctively, I pulled the collar of my shirt up around my ears with a distinct jerk. I buttoned my fishing vest as if it might actually make some difference. "Great weather for August!" The bear grass along the rain-choked river was oily, still heavy and clingy from a massive but slow and steady afternoon downpour, the giver of life in this harsh land. The churning froth in the rapids below Slide Inn, still a pure white after the rain, raced over time-weathered boulders, ebony colored and soapy looking now in the evening light. The sagebrush flats took on a surreal appearance as they extended their sweeping tendrils of sand and scrub, no longer thirsty, toward the more verdant flanks of the great peaks. A part of me wanted to call it off—go back to the cabin and dream of trout by the hearth.

Nevertheless, I still had a ray of optimism left in my soul. I felt sort of, shall we say, sanctified, assured of my ability to strike trout under less than ideal conditions. The big caddis hatches of recent evenings wouldn't come off tonight, I knew. Maybe the caddis knew something about the weather I didn't. The thought briefly crossed my mind that caddis had more brains than I. I quickly dismissed the idea.

"Trichoptera can't reason. I know what I'm doing here."

The conditions were right for some challenging nymph fishing. I intended to prove my worth, or, more likely, try to hone my limited patience with dead drift technique and the Leisenring Lift. A fast bolt of anxiety shot through my stomach, and I resignedly admitted to myself that I'm not the world's greatest nymph fisherman. Then again I had caught a fair share of trout underwater. I became, at least, hopeful.

I selected a nine-foot Winston graphite fly rod for eight-weight line. I tied a dropper to the leader, tied on two nymphs, and weighted the rig heavily with split shot. Above the terminal tackle I had fastened a big fluorescent orange strike indicator, which upon close inspection looked to be proportionately about the size of a basketball. "Only way I can catch the damn things," I muttered, and then forced the thought from my head. With anticipation I flung the heavy rig to the head of a deep run adjacent to the fast current in the middle of the river. I held the rod high, a perfect drift. Nothing. Again I cast with the same result. After about fifteen minutes of this frustration it occurred to me that the usual crowd of Madison River fly-fishers were not out that evening (maybe the caddis had told them something).

In fact, the only other anglers on the stream were a group of four Japanese—a middle-aged man, two teenage boys, and a teenage girl, maybe sixteen years old at most. Soon it became apparent that all of them were catching trout—good trout and at quite a steady rate. I stood there and observed. They all wore faded khaki fishing vests with the words "Japan Flyfishers" emblazoned in a semicircle on the back above the zippered rear pocket. By far the most successful angler in the group was the young girl. I saw her land four rainbows, all over fourteen inches, in the space of forty-five minutes. By this time I had caught two rainbows in the slack water near the bank, both under ten inches. I decided to strike up a conversation.

Although the group was from Tokyo, fortunately for me, they spoke English. I learned that they had come to West Yellowstone to attend the annual Federation of Fly-Fishers Conclave like the rest of us and that this was the first time they had ever fished the Madison. My heart sank. That pesky bolt of anxiety shot through me once again. The girl, I ascertained, was using a big Mono stone fly nymph on her terminal leader with a #14 Gold Ribbed Hare's Ear on the dropper. You can't imagine my anguish when this fact was revealed. I was using exactly the same combination. The girl had caught and released ten nice trout. I had caught two "dinks." Bidding my new friends a rather shaky (and envious) "good luck," I left for the camper. As I drove away I think I unconsciously muttered to myself something sexist like, "Humpf—women."

Since that day I have always been very much aware of women fly-fishers. Like everybody else, I always thought that fly-fishing was basically a "man's sport." I read it in the literature all the time. Perhaps there are more women on the stream today than there were half a century ago, I thought. Certainly there weren't any women anglers to speak of in the nineteenth century. I was wrong. I have since pored over many photographs of early fly-fishers, and it is surprising how many women show up in those pictures. And they are not cooking in the camp, washing clothes, or scraping mud off the men's waders, either. They are fishing, or at least formally posing for a picture with fly rod in hand. I've seen many pictures of women actually fishing, a big wicker creel slung over their shoulder. Propriety was always a concern, for most of these fly-fisherwomen before 1900 wore long, flowing skirts, sometimes hooped, while wading in the stream. Many were decked out in wide-brimmed hats with long, flowing veils to protect their faces from biting insects.

The supposition that there were more than a few women anglers prior to the twentieth century is not really that surprising, especially in the West. Beginning as early as the late 1830s, many women traveled with their husbands and fathers over the Oregon Trail in search of the new Eldorado. Life on the early western frontier was harsh, requiring a division of labor usually apportioned on the basis of physical strength. In many instances family life on the wilderness homestead only reinforced traditional female role prescriptions.

But there were many women who lost their men on the trail or on the farm or ranch. Some historians argue that this figure approaches 20 percent over the course of frontier history. Brooklyn College professor Lillian Schlissel has determined that by the end of the nineteenth century, between 12 and 15 percent of all homesteaders in the West were women living alone, either unmarried or widowed. In more than a few cases, businesswomen actually came west by themselves to open restaurants, hotels and boarding houses, laundries, and of course those inevitable establishments of lesser repute. It is not surprising, therefore, that it was in the West where American women first achieved the right to own their own property. Wyoming became the first democratic political entity in the world where women achieved the right to vote and the right to sit on juries. Other western states quickly followed suit.

As territorial delegations met to draft state constitutions in the nineteenth and twentieth centuries, the male delegates had to face the fact that there were many independent women out there who already owned property and wished to keep it. These women had had to compete with men on their own terms, in a "man's" environment, simply to survive. They had helped build the territories toward statehood as men's equals, and they were not about to relinquish freedoms that were already, of necessity, theirs. If these women plowed, branded, and hunted for food, it is also likely that they fished. The illustrious "Queen of Gamblers," Poker Alice Tubbs, certainly did when her gambling hall in the Black Hills was shut down by the authorities. Frequently she would be seen tramping the hills with rifle and fishing rod, too proud to admit that these forays were a necessity. But the photographic evidence of the past suggests that there were a significant number of women, married and unmarried, who also insisted on fishing for sport—just like the men.

In the Southeast, the old paternal code of southern chivalry and gentility, which kept ladies out of schools and businesses and in the home, restricted the number of women anglers in that region. In the Northeast, after the Civil War, lower-middle-class women began working outside the home, mostly in factories, as they had done during the war. And a few of them began showing up about this time in photographs depicting Catskill camps. How many affluent women from the East went fishing, however, is arguable. Among eastern bluebloods, fly-fishing was still considered to be a man's sport in the 1890s. But in the West, especially in rural areas, the outdoor life seemed to breed more than the usual numbers of women anglers, judging from early journals and photographs.

Still, western women don't seem to have contributed as much to the evolution and development of the sport in the earlier years as their counterparts did in the East. But neither did western men much before the 1920s. Nevertheless, taken as a whole, American women did contribute significantly to the evolution of the sport, especially in the realm of flytying. In so doing, they influenced western fly-fishing to various degrees. Many of us are familiar with the contributions of Mary Orvis Marbury, the only daughter of the great tackle merchant, Charles F. Orvis of Manchester, Vermont. Mary was taught the mysteries of flytying, probably by an Orvis flytier named John Hailey, and thus grew up steeped in the tradition of New England fly-fishing. In 1876, at the age of nineteen, she assumed the responsibility for fly production with the Orvis Company. Orvis was mainly a mail-order concern (and still is), and by the late 1880s Charles was becoming a bit frustrated with meeting customers' demands for fly patterns in a country where fly patterns were not standardized. Mary Marbury changed all that by beginning to name and standardize patterns that previously had only been identified by a number or which had names that were popularly used for several different flies used in various regions throughout the U.S.

In 1892 she published her classic book, *Favorite Flies and Their Histories*, which went a long way in categorizing the gaudy Victorian wet flies popular in that era. The book contained more than 500 pages with stories, anecdotes, and poems contributed by over 200 people, many of whom resided in the West. The book, which sold at the time for five dollars, became one of the landmarks of fly-fishing literature and served the American fly-fisher well until 1935, when Preston Jennings got us thinking in terms of more exact entomological imitation with his monumental work, *A Book of Trout Flies*.

Time and again I have run across descriptions of flies recommended for western streams that can be traced back to *Favorite Flies*, so it's not too ridiculous to assume that the Orvis Company did a respectable mail-order business with western anglers. Many western preferences are listed in the book, including such well known patterns as the Professor, preferred by L.Z. Coman, M.D., of Boulder, Colorado. The venerable Royal Coachman was the favorite of S.H. Green of Portland, Oregon. The most popular fly in the West before the 1920s was undoubtedly the Royal Coachman, a pattern that John Hailey of Orvis developed about 1878. The fly was named by Charles Orvis' brother. The new pattern caught on and was eventually tied both wet and dry. None other than Preston Jennings stated that the fly best imitated the *Isonychia* bicolor, but most anglers agree that it specifically imitates nothing known in nature – it just works. Eventually, it was adapted regionally. The old Gilt (gold ribbed) Coachman was preferred by many Colorado anglers by the turn of the century. The California Coachman is still used on the West Coast, where a bright yellow band is substituted for the traditional red.

Interestingly, Marbury's book helped illuminate the artistic talent of another woman flytier, Sara McBride of Mumford, New York. McBride is credited with developing several popular Victorian fly patterns with names like General Hooker, Quaker, and Tomah Jo. As early as 1876, *Forest and Stream* recognized her as one of the nation's most expert and artistic fly-dressers. Where Marbury was a collator, McBride was an originator.

Women not only were a part of Orvis management, they were important customers as well. One of the earliest surviving Orvis catalogs (#16), published sometime between 1883 and 1892, attested to the fact that the number of women fly-fishers in the U.S. was on the increase when it advertised a curiously heavy nine-foot lancewood rod designed specifically for "ladies."

By the 1920s women throughout the nation had become well established as both flytiers and anglers. Most of the ones who were receiving the greatest attention, however, were still from the East. Carrie Gertrude Stevens of Rangeley, Maine is perhaps the most famous of these women of the early twentieth century. On July 1, 1924, after completing her household chores, Carrie sat down and tied a streamer pattern that would, she hoped, imitate the smelts predominant in the Rangeley Lakes where she lived. To test her new creation, Carrie rigged up a fly rod and promptly went out and caught a six-pound, thirteen-ounce brook trout that won second prize in the *Field & Stream* contest for 1924. The Gray Ghost, as the fly was dubbed, became an instant classic. Today, a bronze plaque has been erected on the shore of one of the Rangeley Lakes to commemorate Mrs. Stevens's accomplishment and recognize her artistic skill as a flytier, which was immense considering that she never used a vise.

Although western women didn't match their eastern counterparts in contributing to the evolution of flytying during the early years, they undoubtedly used their contemporaries' creations when they went fishing. In 1897 Mary Trowbridge Townsend caught a four-pound brown trout from Yellowstone's Firehole River only seven years after that species had been planted in the previously barren water. Her experiences, which she titled "A Woman's Trout Fishing in Yellowstone National Park," appeared on the pages of *Outing Magazine*, volume XX, the next year. From the 1890s forward more and more articles by women were seen in the nation's leading sporting journals.

Consider the story by Minnie Louise Langhorst and her sister

Katie from the January 1918 issue of *Forest and Stream*. These two independent young women from San Francisco spent over four weeks
alone during the summer of 1916 mule packing in the depths of California's Kern River canyon and beyond for the purpose of climbing
Mt. Whitney and fly-fishing for the rare golden trout. Several of the
locals down in the Bishop Valley claimed that the pair were the first
white women ever to go into that country unescorted by men. Minnie later wrote that she and her sister proved "that it is not necessary
for women to forego the pleasure of a vacation to their liking because
of the necessity of going alone. We believed," she said, "that we could
travel through the mountains as well as the average man."

At Kern Lake the women actually supplied a local High Sierra
camp (a permanent summer tent camp run by a proprietor) with fish
for a week. On one occasion the Langhorst women hooked two rainbows at the same instant on "brown hackled flies," both over twenty-
three inches. "The trout broke water and shook its head angrily,"
Minnie Langhorst wrote. "Six times during the next fifteen minutes
this was repeated, on several occasions after I thought I had him in
the net." The fish made several long runs into the middle of the lake,
until finally "he allowed himself to be netted without a struggle, so
completely exhausted was he. It was the largest fish I had ever caught."

After a successful climb of Mt. Whitney, the pair literally climbed
around several waterfalls to reach Golden Trout Creek, where they
found every pool, including the spring at the headwaters, to be "teem-
ing with golden beauties." Using a black ant imitation, the sisters
landed sixteen goldens in twenty minutes on the first day they fished
for them. Moving downstream later in the week, Katie caught a golden
more than twelve inches long, a lunker by modern-day standards in
the southern Sierras. They emerged from the mountains triumphant
a couple of weeks later. In all, these "city girls" had traversed the
backbone of the Sierras, climbed the highest mountain in the U.S.
outside of Alaska, crossed the treacherous Kern River twice, caught
golden trout from several streams, and made their way into "many
rough nooks seldom visited by men." Not a bad fishing trip by anyone's standards.

By 1918 "sportswomen" had become big business. In August of
that year, *Forest and Stream* ran a piece that prescribed the proper attire for the outdoor lady, making sure to point out that true sportswomen's clothes were "far different from 'sport garments' designed

for appearance only." By 1918 outdoor clothing, even for women, had become more practical, although skirts were still appropriate. The author of the article suggested a long, belted fishing jacket of "Forestry Cloth," a "Wading Skirt" of the same material, and a "Basket-Weave Shade Hat, bound and banded in back." By this time leading sporting goods stores and mail-order enterprises throughout the nation were stocking functional outdoor clothing for women. Today, when I go into a fly-fishing specialty shop or an outdoor store, I have to search for several minutes, it seems, just to locate men's clothing.

In 1949 the *Denver Post* reported that there were in excess of 50,000 fisherwomen in my home state of Colorado. That figure has mushroomed since. In the 1980s there are more women fly-fishers than ever before. Many native western women have retained the independent, maverick spirit of their forebears, male and female. Some women still farm and ranch and fish by themselves. I know a young lady in southern Wyoming who is the sole owner of a big ranch originally homesteaded by her family in the late 1880s. She's thirty miles from the nearest post office (mail is delivered once a week by horseback or sleigh), and seventy-five miles from the nearest movie theater. In winter, when the snow is four feet deep and the temperature is forty below zero, the only way out is by helicopter, which she pilots with ease when it is necessary to get winter fodder to helpless livestock. She can ride, rope, and castrate calves with the best cowboys in the state and has even done the rodeo circuit as a barrel racer.

One day might find her down on her knees, blue jeans soaked

with blood, birthing calves and giving them life by blowing warm breath from her mouth into theirs. The next day, on a whim, she might kick off her dung-caked boots, toss the Stetson, grimy with red dust and muddy snow stains, into the closet, put on a black crepe dress, fly a helicopter to Cheyenne, and catch a plane to New York, where she'll lunch at the Waldorf, go shopping at Bloomingdales, catch the latest performance of *Les Misérables*, and be home again in time to gather fresh eggs from the chicken house. She also ties flies in her spare time and can handle a big North Platte trout as well as anyone I have ever met.

No longer can fly-fishing (or anything else for that matter) be considered the exclusive domain of men. Fly-fishermen still far outnumber fly-fisherwomen, but the gap *is* closing. Women anglers have always been with us, contrary to popular opinion. Finally, they are starting to get some deserved recognition. I can only dream of being able to flycast as well as Joan Wulff. I will never be able to tie a fly as expertly as Carrie Stevens or Sara McBride. We men may still outnumber them, but gentlemen, many of the serious women fly-fishers I've met are good—very good. If you don't believe me, just keep your eyes peeled for a petite Japanese girl, probably close to twenty years old now, the next time you fish the Madison River.

High Lakes

Out in western Colorado, past endless vistas of salt sage and prehistoric badlands, there is a wild mountain lake sitting high on a broad volcanic shelf that is almost large enough to be called a valley. It is full of good-sized Colorado River cutthroats and always has been. The setting is resplendent. On the far shore, monolithic flattop peaks, from whence this wilderness derives its name, rise up triumphantly amidst forests of fragrant spruce, lodgepole pine, and shimmering aspen. The mountain peaks here are stratified, their layers of earth and stone exposing successive epochs of the prehistory of this land. With a thin blanket of snow on the broad summits and covering the precipitous shelves below, they remind me of giant frosted layer cakes, chocolate parfaits, and finely tiered Napoleons. To geologists these ancient escarpments read like a book. They tell the story of countless eons of shifting earth, vulcanism, faulting, and massive upheaval.

Indian paintbrush, mountain asters, and wild mushrooms grow around the lake's perimeter. A doe and her fawn, usually surreptitious and hushed in their movements over the thick pine needles of the forest floor, might surprise you as you lie quietly in your sleeping bag. Elk often can be heard in the autumn bugling in the dense stands of timber across the still lake. Presumptuous beavers slap their tails and spray intruders with wet foam in a series of ponds below the outlet, while comical marmots may be seen scurrying around the tundra at the higher elevations.

This natural body of water forms the headwaters of the White River, and for as long as anybody can remember, it has been called Trapper's Lake. The very name conjures up visions of deep primordial

wilderness, steeped in the old ways and habits of *les coureurs de bois.*
On a still night one can almost hear the thump of a buffalo hide drum
and the methodical footbeats of rough, robed figures dancing La
Ginolet around a huge campfire, while pungent pine smoke ascends
in thick spirals to shroud a frigid hunter's moon. The dazzling reflec-
tion from the moon on the mirrored water of the lake has kept me

from sleeping at night, the silhouetted panoply of century-old pines forming the horizon, distinct, against a fluorescent sky. The cry of a loon, real or imagined, can add an eerie refrain to the mystique of this secretive place. The whirr of wild wings can awaken you from slumber and instantly instill a sense that you are, at least for the moment, truly living in harmony with the natural world. The smell of frying bacon, carried on the breeze from an unseen forest camp, can revive the senses on a sunny morning, as it has done for over a century. There are few other places on this planet where I can sense such a feeling of deep wilderness, as if it were an emotion.

The Trapper's Lake experience is the very essence of western fly-fishing. Throughout the Rockies, Sierras, and the Cascade Mountains, hidden like precious jewels waiting to be discovered, the western U.S. is blessed with thousands of trout-filled high lakes. In the Rockies, they are the best places to locate the elusive cutthroat. Many lakes are above the timberline, and trout at these altitudes can be temperamental. Nasty, cold, windy, rain-prone days are usually the best, but there are always exceptions to this rule. It's often difficult to solve angling problems on these lakes and almost impossible to predict them. I guess that's what makes fishing alpine lakes the ultimate challenge, the allure that keeps bringing us back despite frequent disappointment. Many of them (the best ones) are reached only by miles of hiking up precipitous switchbacks and talus slopes. Burdened with a fifty-pound backpack, it can be a challenge just getting to them. Frequently, pack trains of horses or mules can be seen traveling these trails to a distant lake, painting a picture that is the essence of the Old West. The trips can be grueling.

But it's worth it for many. There is no other place quite so mysterious as a high lake, especially if one has never fished it before. I guess the long, grinding hike required to get there has something to do with the mystery. You have a lot of time to think on the trail—to *anticipate*. Usually, you can't even see the lake you are hiking to until you are right on top of it. The last quarter mile is inevitably the steepest, requiring a scramble up a rocky slope to the shoreline. And then you see it, the sun reflected on the ripples, mystical and serene, almost tranquilizing. I know of few other rewards in the mountains quite so thrilling as finally laying down a heavy pack beside the clear waters of one of these remote alpine gems. I once knew a guy who got so excited about fishing high lakes he had never seen before that he actually rigged up his fly rod as he walked the last quarter mile, so that he could approach the shoreline false casting a fly.

The ultimate experience is to reach one of these lakes in the spring just after ice out, a risky business frequently requiring snowshoes and an ability to sense the location of snow-covered trails. As often as not, the lake will still be frozen when you get there. But if you hit it just right, the fishing can be indescribable. I have camped beside high lakes even in summer where I never laid eyes on another human being for the entire stay. At such times I have felt akin to my ancestors in this land, for here was an outdoor experience practically identical to those enjoyed by outdoorsmen of a century ago; high lakes can be like time capsules. Having a whole lake to oneself can instill a feeling of power, of individualism, almost a sense of ownership—and a sense of history. In the total experience of western angling, high lakes, and the rugged journeys required to reach them, have become tradition, a romantic image that has helped stereotype the sportsman's West. There are few, if any, other places in the lower forty-eight states where the angler can catch a fleeting glimpse of wilderness, unchanged from what fishers of a century ago witnessed.

For the less ambitious, Trapper's Lake is one of the best spots in the West to sample the tradition of fly-fishing high lakes for native cutthroat trout. It was at Trapper's Lake, in fact, that scientist David Starr Jordan collected Colorado River cutts in 1889 and later determined them to be a distinct subspecies—*Salmo clarki pleuriticus*. In a way, however, Trapper's is kind of a "cheater," for it can almost be reached by a gravel road running east from the town of Meeker. The hike in from the developed U.S. Forest Service campground is less than a quarter of a mile, although many other productive high lakes in the Flattops Wilderness Area can be reached by trail from Trapper's. Trapper's Lake was not always so accessible. Lewis B. France fished the lake in the early 1880s after an arduous two-day trip from the Glenwood Springs area. France commented on the magnificent evergreens surrounding the lake. He described the inspirational scene with romantic phrases:

> And thus surrounded, locked in from intrusion by these giants, reposes the beautiful lake, ever kissing with its crystal lips the rugged feet of its noble guardians; there is not a ripple on its surface now, and it mirrors its protectors in their garbs of green from base to dizzy summit; the sun just going down lights up the wonderful cliffs high

above me on the left, and that same light is set almost in the centre of the lake, as if to caress the darker shade of its neighbors from the other side. A glorious and loving company it is, dwelling in perfect harmony, but born through travail; the beach is of lava, ground to pebbles and specks of sand in the mill of centuries.

In 1886, a man by the name of W.L. Pattison built three cabins on Trapper's Lake as a sporting lodge for wealthy industrialist John Cleveland Osgood, the president of the controversial Colorado Fuel and Iron Company. Pattison was a rugged outdoorsman and claimed to have been an Indian scout, U.S. marshal, and sheriff. Pattison and his family spent the winter of 1886–1887 in the cabins trapping and ice fishing while surrounded by eleven feet of snow. Two of these cabins remain today, in good condition, and are used during the trout spawning season by members of the Colorado Division of Wildlife. They are still fueled by woodburning stoves and are considered to be among the very few pre-1900 private western sporting lodges that have survived deep into the twentieth century in excellent condition.

The wonderful fishing in Trapper's Lake had attracted some of the most famous sportsmen in the country by the early years of the twenti-

eth century. About 1916, Zane Grey came in from the east by horse-back. He found the experience of fishing Trapper's so charming that he wrote a four-part serialized account of the trip, which was published in *Outdoor Life* during the spring of 1918. Grey's brother R.C., of Yampa, Colorado, was along on the trip. Apparently, he had fished Trapper's Lake before and was familiar with the habits of the Colorado River cutthroats. There was quite a rivalry between the Grey brothers. "To beat me at anything," Zane wrote, "always gave him the most unaccountable, fiendish pleasure."

One afternoon they rigged up their fly rods and headed for the lakeshore. "These are educated trout," remarked R.C. "It takes a skillful fisherman to make them rise. Now anybody can catch the big game of the sea, which is your forte. But here you are N.G. [No Good]. . . . Watch me cast." Faithful to his boast, the "water boiled" on the first cast. R.C. had hooked a "double" on his tandem wet fly rig.

Moving around the lake, the brothers stripped wet flies over visible trout. Zane Grey had caught four nice cutthroats when he heard R.C. shout. Rushing toward his brother, Zane found him standing in the middle of the swift outlet chute with his rod bent over double and most of his line out. R.C. had hooked a trout that weighed several pounds. "See him—down there—in all that white water—see him flash red," R.C. shouted. "Go down there and land him for me. Hurry! He's got all the line!" The Greys had forgotten their landing net.

Zane ran down the outlet stream intent on beaching the big fish after it tired. "I saw the shine of the leader," he wrote. "But I could not reach it without wading in. When I did this the trout lunged out. He looked crimson and silver. [He was so big] I could have put my fist in his mouth."

"Yank him out!" R.C. shouted, either unaware of the likely result or just too excited to consider it. Zane knew that if he grabbed the leader while the fish was still lithe, he would lose it instantly. Finally, the big cutthroat tired, or so Zane Grey thought, and he attempted to beach it. R.C. came running down the stream panting and exhausted to where his brother was sitting, holding the broken leader in his hand.

By the 1930s a gravel road had been pushed up the White River from Meeker. During the early part of that decade Ray Bergman fished Trapper's Lake for the first time. His party reached the lake by automobile, and they stayed at Trapper's Lake Lodge, a rustic sportsman's hostelry that is still in operation today. Writing in *Trout* in 1938, Bergman stated that Trapper's Lake was one of the best "ponds for fly fishing" that he had ever seen. Like the Greys before him, Ray Bergman soon learned the ways of cruising western cutthroats. "It didn't take me long . . . to find out what it was all about," he wrote. "You didn't fish promiscuously. You did more observation than you did casting, but when you did cast, it was to a rising fish."

Bergman and his party used bucktails, wet flies, and dry flies, all with much success. Writing in *Trout*, he detailed his experience with one particularly memorable fish and one of his favorite flies:

> One good specimen fooled around my location for an hour before I got him. He would look over each one of my offerings, coming right up to each one as if he had decided to take it and then go back to his swimming level with an impudent flip of his tail. One of the most effective flies for me had been the Royal Coachman. The one I had been using was badly chewed up. I went back to the Royal, but selected a new fly instead of the bedraggled specimen. After tying it on I couldn't resist taking one more try at the big fellow, especially as at this time he was lazily swimming by me. I dropped the fly about two feet in front of his line of progress. To my surprise he rose and took it deeply as if it was just what he wanted. Was the new Royal the reason for his change of mind? I don't know, and your guess is as good as mine.

Trapper's Lake has been compared to Yellowstone Lake, and in many respects the analogy is a good one. Through effective scientific management, the fish in Trapper's Lake remain today the largest wild population of Colorado River cutts in the world. That is why the Division of Wildlife strips eggs from the spawning females every spring. The female trout are returned to the lake unharmed, and the eggs are shipped to a state hatchery in Glenwood Springs, Colorado. A year later, the four-inch fingerlings are stocked by airplane into approximately 140 high lakes throughout the state. Many of the cutthroats I catch in the Indian Peaks Wilderness Area, near my home in Boulder, originally came from spawn taken from Trapper's Lake.

In addition, catch-and-release regulations have improved the quality of fishing in Trapper's Lake itself. Fishing is restricted to flies and lures only, and all fish between eleven and sixteen inches must be released. The average-size fish is about fourteen or fifteen inches. There are still some really big ones, however. I once saw a ten-pounder, caught about 1976, hanging on the wall of the Trapper's Lake Lodge. To protect spawning beds, fishing is prohibited in the inlets and outlets. With that restriction, at least, no one will be able to repeat R.C. and Zane Grey's ungainly performance (in the outlet, at least) of years earlier.

As high lakes go, Trapper's is remarkably consistent fishing right through the fall when the elk hunters take over (one of the largest elk herds in Colorado roams the Flattop Wilderness). It's a good spot to introduce a youngster to fishing high lakes with a high probability of success. Later though, you will inevitably want to explore the more remote alpine lakes of the West. You may even have them all to yourself, where only you can hear the thunder of a mountain shower resounding through timberline cliffs, or see an eagle soaring high overhead, reflected in the gin-clear water. Then you will experience one little slice of the unconstrained life known to our ancestors in the West.

The Grand Old Man
of the Wind Rivers

Back in 1948, high on Wyoming's continental divide, an angler by the name of C.S. Read caught a California golden trout weighing eleven and a quarter pounds and measuring twenty-eight inches. The record golden was taken from an alpine lake deep in the rugged wilderness of the Wind River Mountains. On the west side of Yellowstone National Park, during the same year, Charles Brooks caught his first brown trout of over three pounds in the Firehole River. An eleven-pound trout, native only to the Sierras but caught in an isolated Wyoming high lake, is remarkable when you stop to think about it. So is a three-pound brown from the upper Firehole when you consider how maddeningly selective the fish in that stream can be. Fishing for big browns in the Firehole and fishing for elusive goldens anyplace can separate the men from the boys. But at least there's always the chance of success. And there certainly is the challenge. During the 1880s, despite the fact that angling pressure was largely nonexistent, there wouldn't even have been the chance. Prior to 1889 it would have been a lead pipe cinch that you'd catch absolutely nothing from either of these aforementioned places. Both fisheries were completely barren and always had been! Waterfalls were responsible, not man's negligence.

In 1889, one Captain F.A. Boutelle, an enthusiastic angler, decided to alter that situation in the western portion of Yellowstone National Park. He wrote:

> In passing through the park I noticed with surprise the barrenness of most of the water in the park. Besides the beautiful Shoshone and other smaller lakes there are hundreds of miles of as fine streams as any in existence without a fish of any kind. I have written to Col.

Marshall McDonald, U.S. Fish Commission, upon the subject, and have received letters from him manifesting a great interest. I hope through him to see all these waters so stocked that the pleasure-seeker in the Park can enjoy fine fishing within a few rods of any hotel or camp."

Apparently Colonel McDonald was a man of action, because in August and September of that very year (1889), the barren waters of Yellowstone were first stocked with brook trout, Loch Laven, rainbows, blackspotted cutthroats, and mountain whitefish. In 1890, the first generation of browns, which established the population from which Charles Brooks caught three-pounders over half a century later, were introduced into the upper Firehole River.

In waters where indigenous cutthroats already existed, the planting of exotics brought devastating results for the native trout, but where exotics were planted into formerly barren waters, the results were largely beneficial for sportsmen. Today, there are a greater number of productive fisheries available to the angler than ever before, and we can catch almost any kind of trout we wish, depending upon location.

During the last two decades of the nineteenth century, and generally up to the 1930s, few of these exotic stockings were strictly regulated. The U.S. Fish Commission was responsible for stocking federal lands, and in regions of the West that had attained statehood, state commissions might try to regulate trout propagation and stocking. But in the territories, and in local regions everywhere, private individuals and groups were pretty much free to dump a bucketful of trout anywhere they wished—with the blessing of local government.

These early stockings accomplished two goals, one of them bad and one of them good. First, exotics replaced native cutthroats in many depleted waters. Second (and this is the good one), these stockings nearly doubled, in some locales, the number of streams and lakes that could be utilized by anglers. Unfortunately, natives were not replaced with natives in historic watersheds. Like everything else, it was a matter of economics (rainbows could be raised more efficiently, and browns and brookies could establish breeding populations quite readily). Even if cutthroats had been propagated by government commissions for planting in native fisheries, the lack of regulation in respect to who could stock and who couldn't, and the fact that there were hundreds of square miles devoid of game wardens, makes it unlikely that such populations would have survived. Considering that many anglers of the Gilded Age thought it desirable to make available as many different kinds of trout as possible (and this is still a desirable goal for many today), it is doubtful that the cutthroat could have been restored adequately throughout its historic range.

The most intriguing human interest stories surrounding these early stocking programs involve the efforts of private individuals. As is so often the case, most of these people were anglers interested in improving the quality of their sport. Today, one of the best fly-fishing opportunities available in the Rocky Mountains is centered just east of the little town of Pinedale, Wyoming, in the heart of the Wind River Mountains; right up there where that big golden trout was caught in 1948. The Wind Rivers were, and still remain, one of the most isolated mountain ranges in the West. Most of the early wagon trains to California and Oregon missed them completely. Their most visible role in western history was during the fur trade era and just after, between 1820 and 1860, when the great valley below these majestic peaks rang to shouts of drunken trappers during the spring rendezvous. The Wind Rivers also inspired the paint brush of Albert Bierstadt. During the 1880s and right into the early years of the twentieth century, cattlemen and sheepherders fought over these mountains. During the early 1900s they were still mostly uninhabited wilderness, far off the beaten path.

It was at this time that a young boy by the name of Finis Mitchell came out with his parents from Missouri to live near the base of the Wind River Mountains. The Mitchells' homestead was on a tract of sage and dust near the Big Sandy entrance to what is today the Bridger Wilderness. The hopeful little family pulled up to their new home on April 26, 1906, with "a span of mules, a wagon, and a cow. [All] our worldly possessions were in that wagon and on our backs," Finis Mitchell reminisced. Three years later the boy climbed his first of what eventually totaled some 200 mountain peaks in the Wind River Range, and a lifelong love affair with the wilderness had begun. In 1923, Finis took a job with the Union Pacific Railroad in Rock Springs, but was laid off on March 4, 1930, when the Great Depression tightened its grip on the people of Wyoming. Finis had a wife, Emma, to support at this time, so he returned to the mountains and started trapping in an attempt to make a living.

The pioneers of Wyoming have always had to be innovative and

resourceful to survive in that harsh land. Within three months after his return to his beloved Wind River Mountains, Finis and his wife bought a big canvas tent, borrowed ten worn-out horses and a few beat up riding and pack saddles from some friendly ranchers, and opened "Mitchell's Fishing Camp" on Mud Lake. An old potbellied cookstove was set up in one corner of the tent. A bed was squeezed into another corner. Emma did the cooking, and she was famous "throughout the entire mountain range." Her specialty was cake, baked in a dutch oven. The Mitchells charged a dollar and a half a day for each horse. They kept a dollar and gave the fifty cents to the ranchers who had loaned them the horses. Meals were fifty cents. The guide service Mitchell provided, and he "made sure [clients] caught their fish," was free of charge (things certainly have changed, haven't they?). During the first summer of operation Finis and Emma Mitchell made $300.15. For the next seven years anglers would drive their Model A pickups into Mitchell's Fishing Camp to sample the local sport.

Finis Mitchell's biggest problem when he opened his business was that the number of lakes in the Wind River Mountains that had fish in them could be tabulated on one hand. Like the western part of Yellowstone National Park and elsewhere, many of the high lakes in the Wind Rivers had always been barren of trout because precipitous waterfalls prevented the upstream migration of the native cutthroats. Finis Mitchell decided to change all that. He rigged up two five-gallon "coal oil cans," with the tops cut out. He made wooden lids for the cans, hauled them on horseback to Big Sandy Lake, and then proceeded to catch seventeen small cutthroats. The fish were deposited into the cans and then packed over to barren Rapid Lake. Along the way the horses were frequently halted so that the cans could be "shaken up" in order to oxygenate the water and keep the trout alive. The seventeen cutts were planted in Rapid Lake and were left undisturbed.

One day, two years later, Finis and his father went up to Rapid Lake to find out the result of their experiment. Right away, Finis caught a three-and-a-half-pound cutthroat, a big buck. Finis released the fish, because for all he knew, there might have only been one male in that original group of seventeen. Soon, however, there was cause for real optimism. Finis proceeded around the lake and caught another male weighing in at five-and-a-half pounds. He kept this fish, had it mounted, and placed it on display in the window of Mike Dankowski's sporting goods store. Business at the fishing camp increased dramatically.

One fine morning in 1933, Finis took his two fish cans over the continental divide to Grave Lake where mackinaw trout had once been stocked. It took his group most of the day, so they camped by the lake that night. Their objective was to catch some "small" mackinaw for restocking. According to Mitchell, "all we could catch were big ones." Consequently, only three fish, weighing about three pounds each, made the trip back over the divide in the oil cans. Finis planted them in an unnamed lake they dubbed May Lake. A few years later an employee of Finis Mitchell's caught a ten-and-a-half-pound mackinaw from May Lake. More than half a century later, mackinaw can still be caught there. Eventually, a State of Wyoming hatchery agreed to provide Finis Mitchell with trout fry if he would stock the barren lakes in the Wind River Mountains. He jumped at the chance.

No fancy airplane drops for Mitchell. Hatchery personnel would deliver the trout in five-gallon milk cans, twelve cans at a time—rainbows, cutthroats, goldens, brookies, and browns. Finis and his father would haul the fish to remote, barren lakes on the backs of six pack horses. They received no financial compensation for their services other than increased business for the fishing camp. It is estimated that between 1930 and 1937, Finis Mitchell was responsible for stocking two and a half million trout into 314 Wind River high lakes. Today, anglers are still catching trout that are descendant from Mitchell's original stocks.

In 1937, Finis Mitchell returned to Rock Springs and the Union Pacific Railroad. He visited the Wind River Mountains often, though, to fish and to climb the great peaks, including one that now bears his name. There are very few people who have loved these mountains as much as Finis Mitchell did; he has come to be known in Wyoming as "The Grand Old Man of the Mountains." Poet, philosopher, naturalist, and sportsman, Mitchell expressed his love for the land many times through the years. His main concern from the beginning was the preservation of the wilderness for the enjoyment of others. He wrote:

> May you always camp where waters run clear
> Within serene valleys of flowers and shade,
> Where well trod trails of friendship meet
> And your kindness and grace never fade.

Today, a fly-fisher can pack into the Wind River Mountains and cast a nymph or dry fly to goldens, cutthroats, rainbows, browns, and brookies while camped beside jeweled waters. He or she may never lay eyes on another human for a week. The fishing in these mountains is recognized as some of the most productive in the entire West. Summer business in Pinedale, Wyoming, flourishes because of the sport; a sport made possible, largely, by the efforts of Finis Mitchell. The hand of man is not always detrimental to the angling environment. Indeed, it may be vitally necessary today if we are going to preserve our fisheries for future generations. Although the "pure" environmentalist might logically disagree, preferring instead the wilderness as it always was, even to the extent of preserving barren waters, as a fly-fisher it's sort of nice to know that a few places actually exist where you and I can pitch our tent in deep wilderness, under the shadow of great peaks, and relish a fly-fishing experience unknown even to our pioneer ancestors.

The Finest Rod in Colorado Territory

I think I was fourteen when my father presented me with the old fly rod. He said it was sort of an heirloom, passed down through the family from an ancestral uncle, "Major" Daniel Vanderslice. The Major, it seems, had been something of a dignitary, appointed by President Franklin Pierce as the first agent for the Sauk and Fox Indian tribes in the newly established Kansas Territory of 1854. Supposedly, Daniel had acquired the rod from a busted prospector on his way back to Missouri from the Colorado goldfields in the early 1860s. That made the rod almost 100 years old when I was a kid. Daniel had been traveling to Denver City at the time to see what the gold rush was all about. According to my father, who learned the story from his father, Vanderslice had purchased the fly rod from the prospector somewhere on the Smokey Hill Trail as the two men crossed paths during their journeys.

It was a homemade job and not very pretty. To tell you the truth, as a kid of fourteen, I was really self-conscious about fishing with the funny looking thing. "Where did ya get that old clunker?" was the common taunt from my peers. Consequently, I preferred using a twelve-dollar Wright-McGill fiberglass model that I had found under our tree the previous Christmas. The old fly rod was a ten-footer; the butt had been constructed from some soft wood that had darkened with age. The tip obviously had been replaced sometime during the rod's history, and the whole thing was housed in a musty smelling, mildewed cloth sack that was, maybe, thirty years old. It had a hickory grip made from a buggy-whip handle, which tapered down to a hand-sanded reel seat that was merely a continuous extension of the grip. The ferrules and guide rings were large and looked as though they had been forged by caring hands rather than mass-produced in some inadequately ventilated, second-story New England factory during America's age of industrialization after the Civil War. The willowy tip was simply too limber to pick up line effectively, though. The rod had no backbone. It looked like the inexpensive lancewood models advertised in turn-of-the-century Sears or Montgomery Wards catalogs. The old fly rod was really too fragile and inadequate to fish with much enthusiasm.

Despite its history, Dad hadn't wanted it. He only did a little fishing, and that was when he had been a younger man. I don't ever remember going with him to a stream or lake. That task was left to my uncle, whom I accompanied on several trips each year. Uncle Bill taught me the basics of casting and fishing with the fly. I do have a yellowing old photograph of my father fishing with that rod, however, snapped sometime during the 1930s with a Kodak Brownie. He was landing a small trout on Colorado's South Boulder Creek. The picture is a real classic. My dad was decked out with pipe, fedora, wicker creel – the whole works. I only fished the old rod a few times, usually in the company of my uncle on some Ozark spring creek, and only then if there were no other kids around. I would cast a big, yellow Wooly Worm to the head of a long, slick pool while Uncle Bill stood knee deep in the stream behind me supervising my attempts to impart action to the fly by jerking up the rod tip at regular intervals while simultaneously stripping in slack line. I do remember catching a few fish with the antique, but not very many. My 1950s Perrine automatic fly reel (the kind that would land your fish and fillet it immediately on the rod tip if you pressed the retrieval button too hard) was simply too heavy to achieve adequate rod balance on my eclectic rig.

Anyway, I never used the rod much when fishing by myself or with friends. The relic wasn't considered especially valuable by my family, and my father never checked up on me to see if I was caring for it adequately – so I didn't. I was just too young to be trusted with such an heirloom. Today, I know only too well that the rod should probably be hanging on the wall of the American Museum of Fly Fishing in Manchester, Vermont. I realize I probably could have retired from the proceeds of its sale to a collector. My only defense, and it's a poor one, is that as a teenager I didn't begin to realize the rod's importance. To me, at the time, it was just plain "ugly." So I loaned it to a friend for his visiting cousin to use, and I never saw it again. I think they probably broke it, but they made up a series of lame excuses revolving around the idea that the rod was left on a streambank somewhere, and when they went back to retrieve it, it was gone–"stolen," they claimed. After I realized that my father was not going to kill me for losing the rod, I never gave the unfortunate incident a second thought–until a few years ago.

While doing some routine research on Colorado's pioneers, I came upon a startling article in a turn-of-the-century western travel magazine. The article was written by L.B. France, one of Denver's first attorneys, who came west from Illinois to join the Colorado gold rush in 1861. France was an avid fly-fisher and would go to extreme lengths to enjoy his sport. The article traced his reminiscences of angling in the foothills of the Rockies during the late 1800s.

Before the coming of the railroads, the early gold camps depended solely on the arrival of provisions by ox team from Missouri. Bacon, flour, and mining equipment took priority over luxuries on the freighter's wagons, which crossed the dusty plains annually from Westport on the 600-mile journey to Denver City. Fly rods were not considered essential articles of merchandise. Consequently, France made his first rod from local materials. While cooped up in his crude Denver cabin during the cold first months of 1862, the young lawyer whiled away the dreary days fashioning his rod. He used, "a piece of pine for the butt; cedar straight grained and without flaw, for the second joint and tip. A well selected hickory buggy-whip handle furnished the timber for the grip. A jack knife, glass and sand paper served for tools." The handcrafted rod was a ten-footer. For mountings, France had neither tools nor metal, so he engaged a local "tinker of watches" to fit him out with "two sets of ferrules and a half dozen guide rings for the modest sum of seven dollars in gold dust."

Saloons and drugstores appeared on the early frontiers of the West with considerable alacrity, so L.B. France did not have to look far for "oil, shellac, and alcohol" to clean and finish his rod after the hardware was wrapped. Finally, he "strung that rod together," and in the privacy of their cabin, "submitted it to the inspection of the madam." She pronounced it to be "just perfect, the finest rod in Colorado Territory." During that winter the fly rod was subjected to weekly examinations and comment. Thoughts of using it during the coming

summer became "prime subjects of evening conversation over the kitchen stove," France remembered. "There had never been, nor could there ever be vouchsafed to any other couple the amount of enjoyment banked up and ready to draw upon, than was stored away during that memorable winter, and the rod was the pole star . . . everything pointed to it."

Unfortunately, L.B. France used his "marvel of excellence and beauty," as he called it, only a few times. "The rod was too good to keep," he sadly reported. "I lost it early, just like the good children die young." It seems the attorney loaned his rod to a friend, a man named Sam. Sam promised to return the rod in perfect condition after a week-long trip to South Boulder Creek. A month later Sam knocked at the door of the France cabin. Upon entering, Sam held his hat in his hand, and he was slightly trembling. "About that fishing rod," he said. "The fact is I found an old friend on South Boulder, and he took such a fancy to that rod, that I could do no less than make him a loan of it." The man's name was Joshua, Sam sheepishly reported, but he had recently left to "go back to the states," and the rod was now hopelessly lost. Denver City was not a very ceremonious community in those days, though it was kindly disposed. France considered telling Sam to "say his shortest prayer if he [had] more than one," but changed his mind and stoically told his friend "not to say any more about it." That summer L.B. France fished "with a clear conscience and a plum-bush pole and had a good time."

Almost two decades later Sam knocked on the France door once again. By this time the young gold rush lawyer had made a name for himself sorting out local mining customs and translating them into legislation that would become territorial law. He had served as Denver's first prosecuting attorney and become clerk to the House Judicial Committee in Colorado's first territorial legislature. But all his accomplishments in public office could not have made L.B. France happier than he was on that day when his old friend Sam presented him with a new hexagonal split-bamboo rod with German silver mountings and machine-made handle. Sam had recently traveled to the East by rail and purchased the new rod from the prestigious firm of Hiram Leonard. For good measure he had also purchased his friend a reel, one of the revolutionary new Orvis perforated, single-action models with nickel plating that was patented in 1874. Remembering how sorry Sam had been about the loss of the homemade rod, L.B.

France was extremely touched. Recalling the joys of the old rod, he said, "I never felt just exactly the same way but once before . . . and when my generous friend put into my hands [that] miracle of grace and artistic skill, the old feeling came back and I was two inches taller."

Yes. I was amazed by the article when I read it, to say the least. In fact, I had to read it three times just to be sure it was for real. I photocopied it and took it home with me. I was filled with anticipation because something in the recesses of my brain kept nagging at me. I remembered the personal papers of my ancestral uncle, Major Daniel Vanderslice, stashed away in my files. There was one letter in particular, not one of the original documents in his estate, but rather an item I had picked up through sheer serendipity some years before. I had thought at the time that the letter might have something to do with the old fly rod I had lost as a boy. Searching through my files, I located the document. It was an old letter signed by a Mr. T.A. Probst, esq., a secretary for the Nemaha Indian Agency in Highland, Kansas where Daniel Vanderslice had been agent. The letter was addressed to a gentleman in Denver City. The man's last name was partially obliterated by a water stain, probably the result of a summer thunderstorm on the wild Kansas prairie. Nevertheless, the first name of the recipient of the aged letter was clearly visible. It was "Joshua."

Although some of the writing had been obscured by time and the elements, one segment stood right out and slapped me across the face. The statement was in reference to Joshua's impending journey back to the Missouri River that very summer. It read:

> As I previously informed you in my last correspondence, Maj. Vanderslice will meet you far down on the Plains, perhaps as far as Council Grove and there to purchase from you, Sir, what provisions you have remaining that he might be in need of; as he wishes not to be burdened with numerous provisions for the entire duration of the journey to the [gold] fields.

The letter was dated June 6, 1862. Now, as a professional historian, committed to exact and unbiased research, I cannot without doubt assert that Daniel Vanderslice purchased a fly rod from that Joshua fellow. Neither can I conclude that, if he did, it was the same rod once lovingly created by L.B. France. But I will go so far as to say that it is entirely possible. "Joshua" was the name Sam gave to L.B. France as the man who had returned to the States with the rod.

Certainly from France's description, his rod and mine were quite similar. And they originated in the same place, that's pretty certain.

It really doesn't make any difference in the long run. At least the two fly rods, if they were indeed not one and the same, did have a somewhat parallel history. Insofar as I can ascertain, they were practically identical in construction, and ironically, France and I both lost our rods early, "just like the good children die young." I don't seriously regret having lost the rod even now that I possibly know something of its history. I am not a serious collector of old rods, although I do have a low-serial-numbered Orvis Battenkill split-bamboo that

I plan to pass on when I can no longer use it. I still probably wouldn't use the old rod if I had it—even if its monetary value were nil. When I am seriously intent on catching trout, I want to use the most reliable equipment available.

No, what is important to me, I guess, is not the artifacts themselves, so much as the values that can be learned from them. What is really important about that old rod is that it symbolized what life was like on the frontier. Cut off from civilization, the pioneers who opened any new land were forced to utilize whatever local materials and resources they had available to sustain life. Nature provided for many of their needs, and innovation, adaptation, and creativity provided for the rest. These skills helped to mold a culture that still esteems certain qualities of frontier individualism as basic values. That old rod was the very essence of harsh realities experienced by individuals living on the raw western frontier. It can tell us something about the people and their needs, desires, dreams, and goals.

L.B. France would not let the conditions of the environment prevent him from pursuing his favorite sport at any cost. With only an amateur's knowledge, he crafted a fly rod, innovating and adapting available materials the best he could in its construction. And that is why he so appreciated the skilled, professional craftsmanship of the fine Leonard rod when it was presented to him by his friend Sam. The trappings of culture and civilization, symbolically represented here by a new split-bamboo fly rod, reached the frontier through the ambitions and efforts of people like L.B. France. And that was *the* goal as far as the pioneers were concerned—to create a civilized life like they had known back east.

France's published article was accompanied by a photograph of himself standing on a rock beside South Boulder Creek in a little canyon I frequently fish, more than a century later. His left hand is in the pocket of his tweed coat, his right arm is stiffly extended, proudly, like a Greek statue, gripping what was undoubtedly his fine bamboo rod, a man just like me, relishing the accomplishments of his civilization and the trappings of his sport.

Western Campfires

There are few experiences in life as tranquil and gratifying as those moments spent in the deep woods watching the glowing embers of a campfire on a dark night. The pungent aroma of woodsmoke penetrates your clothes. Pine logs crackle and pop while sparks shoot upward, spiral, and then fade into the blackness. The dense outline of the primeval forest, ever so faintly defined in the firelight, casts a spell that is timeless and unique no matter how often the scene is witnessed. One thinks deep thoughts at such times—satisfying thoughts of big trout and a good day on the stream—images that will be etched in the memory for a lifetime. For these brief moments, perhaps, we feel completely integrated with nature; time seems to have no meaning, and the problems of everyday living are far away. There is nothing especially "western" about camping out—here is a tradition that transcends regionalism. I just can't think of a better place to do it than in the great western mountains.

The very act of camping can evoke a sense of tidiness in the most hopeless ragamuffin. Pitching the tent, spreading out the sleeping bags, and placing the fire or cooking ring becomes an honored ritual. The desired view from the tent flap is always considered at length. Never, never do we emerge, sleepy-eyed, from our cozy abode only to catch a glimpse of the family station wagon in the golden morning light. Our fishing gear and cooking utensils are neatly arranged. Dead firewood is neatly stacked. If we are in the backcountry, our backpacks are carefully stuffed with unsightly junk that would be aesthetically displeasing if viewed lying around on the ground. Meticulously, we arrange our camps to look just like the ones in the pages of *Field*

& Stream — it's mandatory. If we don't give ourselves the impression that we look like Mark Trail, or at least some guy from the cover of a vintage L.L. Bean catalog, then we think we've failed.

We'll brew up a cup of coffee or tea in a well-used pot and then squat — not sit — beside the open fire and carefully poke the embers with a long stick — sort of like a cowboy at branding time. Somewhere I read that certain psychologists think camping, fishing, and hunting dispel the urge among grown men to "play cowboy" in a more socially acceptable way. Maybe that's true. But don't get me wrong, I am not one of those guys who heads to the woods with only one blanket and a sack of jerky in order to see what it was like in the age of the mountain men. I like my featherweight nylon tent and three-season goose down sleeping bag as much as I like casting a strong-backboned graphite fly rod. Every time I think how great it would have been to live in the nineteenth century, I just remind myself what a trip to the dentist would have been like in those days.

Nevertheless, for many, me included, there is a certain age-old tradition and mystique surrounding the experience of camping out. We might take along a treasured heirloom from days gone by, an old knife our grandfather gave us, perhaps a vintage coffee pot, the kind that's midnight blue with little white speckles on the enamel finish. I remember my first tent, an old green canvas job my dad ordered from the Sears catalog — you know, the kind that smells like old-fashioned insect repellent. It only took about eight hours to set up, fit just right in the back seat of a car (the whole back seat), and didn't weigh the vehicle down at all — providing the vehicle in question was a long-nosed Kenworth. Still, I treasured that tent, and I can assure you it would still be in use had the termites not devoured it some years back.

Recently, a good friend of mine surprised me with a vintage 1920s (or 1930s?) patent Coleman camp stove for a Christmas present. It looks much like the modern Colemans sans all the lightweight space-age metals. The fuel tank alone on the old stove weighs as much as an anvil, and a person can get a hernia just trying to pump it up. Nevertheless, I can't help but wonder how many fishing trips it has seen. Did it find service on a familiar trout stream long before I was born? What was the fishing like on that stream when the stove was new? I can stare at it all day and fantasize. It will go with me on many trips in the future, right along with my vintage single burner, fire-engine-

red Coleman gas lantern and an old teapot which, by the way, I once used to match a *callibaetis* hatch by examining specimens floating around on the water inside. But these relics won't show up in my backpack. Only the most modern lightweight conveniences travel with me to the backcountry.

During the 1960s and 1970s backpacking and the backpacking industry took off in full force. It has cooled down a little in the 1980s, but it is still viable. Today we have integrated all the elements of high technology to make our hikes in the wilderness more comfortable. We have lightweight aircraft aluminum, ripstop nylon, Thinsulate, Gore-Tex; the list goes on forever. I find it somewhat ironic that except for goose down, most of these synthetic innovations came about as a result of the great "back to the land" movement of the '60s. Nevertheless, the stuff is good, and you can still get so carried away with the new products that you run the risk of falling into the "equipment trap." It can get expensive. It's not my intention here to recommend specific items or products to take to the wilderness. There are plenty of books in print currently filling that need. My best advice is to just go light when backpacking.

The concept of "going light" is not a modern fad. In fact, it's not new at all. For a long time I assumed our ancestors routinely hauled cast-iron stoves into the wilderness by buckboard and set them up in their heavy canvas wall tents. Not so! In fact, campers were finding ways to conserve weight over a century ago. Undoubtedly, the originator and first prophet of "going light" was George Washington Sears, better known to three decades of *Forest and Stream* readers as "Nessmuk." During the post–Civil War decades this flamboyant, bearded sportsman enchanted scores of Americans with his tales of the deep woods and the comparative attributes of various camping paraphernalia. He probably did more than any single sporting writer to shape the concept and mystique of "camping out." Reputedly, he would leave for a week's outing with only a couple of tin dishes, a small muslin tent, a blanket, and a pocket axe. He boasted that his whole outfit for a week, including food and fishing gear, weighed only twenty-six pounds, and he openly ridiculed anyone taking heavy equipment or even heavy clothes into the woods. Nessmuk himself weighed only 105 pounds.

By the 1880s Nessmuk was something of a national celebrity. This guy didn't always hide out in the woods picking old nymph shucks off the willow bushes beside a trout stream either. In fact, he enjoyed the limelight considerably, liking nothing more than to paddle his canoe up to the dock of some fashionable Adirondack resort where wealthy patrons would keep him well lubricated with Creme de Menthe frappes, or whatever else people drank in those places during the 1880s, and spin yarns and give advice till midnight. Always, he encouraged campers to "go light." For generations now, Nessmuk's little book *Woodcraft* has helped shape the whole ambiance of living in the woods.

Unfortunately, the title of Nessmuk's book is all too revealing regarding the attitudes of most nineteenth-century campers toward live trees. For a society that generally was familiar with living close to the land, going camping for a two-week period or more was commonplace. Many consumptives in the Rocky Mountains camped out for several months at a stretch. These so-called "permanent camps," set up for several weeks or more, have given us the impression that *all* Victorian sportsmen carted everything including the kitchen sink into the woods. During the middle years of the nineteenth century, it was common practice to chop live branches and limbs from trees to fashion elaborate shelters, almost cabin-like in construction, or for use as sleeping pads. If the lumber industry was unregulated, which it was at the time, it seemed perfectly appropriate for sportsmen to fell a tree or two on a camping trip. The wood axe was considered a more important item than a tent or sleeping blanket.

Today, of course, this practice is totally unacceptable. In many regions of the West, it is not even permissible to build campfires using dead and downed timber. Fires can scar the tundra for years, and they make frequently visited or "designated" camping spots unsightly. Fortunately, the experience of the Civil War helped to alleviate the situation if only to a slight degree. After 1865, there were suddenly scores of canvas Sibley tents on the surplus market. Men had grown accustomed to living in these customized tepees during the war. Canvas was relatively inexpensive. Right through the early decades of the twentieth century, then, tents became the mode, although green timber was still utilized (and recommended) for such things as tent poles, sleeping pads, and starting fires. As late as 1915, *Forest and Stream* readers were advised to "live off the natural resources of the land as far as possible," while camping.

A *Forest and Stream* article dated July 1917 advised campers to use "green logs" for cooking. The article was accompanied by several illustrations of different types of campfires, each utilizing tree limbs, and large green logs as a basis for the cook fire. There was the "Old-Style Crane," which featured cooking pots hung from a green limb (so that it would not burn) and supported by two forked limbs. The "Permanent Fire-Back" required cutting heavy green logs to support long-lasting smoldering coals between them. Ironically, the same article illustrated a "Handy Pocket Stove" consisting of three twelve-inch "strap-hinges" (the kind that were used on doors of sheds and barns) held together with a small bolt. The innovation looks remarkably like a modern lightweight backpacking grill. The contraption still required a campfire underneath it, however, and "green twigs" were recommended. For all the concern for conservation (including sound forestry practices) advocated by *Forest and Stream*, the idea that a nation full of sportsmen could do real damage to the woods apparently did not occur to the publication's editors during the early years of the twentieth century.

At least the use of tents helped save trees. Or did it? During the later decades of the nineteenth century and the early decades of the twentieth, the classic canvas wall tent came to replace the old army Sibleys. The wall tent quite simply became an institution in the camping industry during these years. Here was the roomy, tall-standing, easily heated home in the backwoods that was perhaps the most practical form of shelter ever devised for long-term camping. If you take a guided horse pack trip to some remote high lake in the West, it is very likely that your guide will still set up a heated wall tent for your comfort. In the early 1920s, the *Field & Stream Outdoorsman's Handbook* recommended wall tents ranging in size from seven-and-a-half feet by seven-and-a-half feet for two people up through twelve feet by thirteen-and-a-half feet. The standard camping tents ranged in weight from ten pounds for the two-person models to twenty-four pounds for the larger camping versions. There were, of course, giant-sized wall tents built for permanent logging camps.

Wall tents were designed to take stoves in one end, which could keep the camper comfortable for several weeks at a time. An old cast-iron stove might find its way into the woods with one of these canvas monsters, but by the early twentieth century, sheet-metal stoves were being constructed especially for these tents. The major drawback to wall tents, however, was their sheer weight and bulk. Consequently, most sportsmen didn't add to their load by carrying poles into the

woods with them; they relied instead on green tree limbs. Commented
the editors of the *Outdoorsman's Handbook*, "those who carry tent poles
don't know the game." Green limbs were preferable to dead ones,
since their resiliency was needed when the sides of the tent were
stretched and made taut. A ridgepole over the top of the tent was
necessary as well as crossed "shear" poles on each end. As many as
ten guy lines on each side were stretched out and tied to flanking
ridgepoles on the sides that were as long as the tent itself. Unavoid-
ably, pitching a wall tent required cutting green tree limbs during the
days before telescoping aluminum tent poles.

Smaller "Canoe Tents," "Baker Tents," which featured a veranda
flap for cooking in rainy weather, and the so-called "Forester Tents,"
the forerunner of modern backpacking tents, also required long ridgepoles or shears. One unique model during the '20s, the "Automobile
Tent," was a mark of progress. It only required a single eight-foot pole
in front. Its rear corners were "guyed out to the body of an automobile." Sheet-metal tent stoves ranged in size from ten by eleven by
eighteen feet to ten by twelve by thirty-two feet. They were regularly
made without a bottom, being intended to sit on a stone hearth and
to fold up into a flat parcel for transportation.

In the backcountry, however, campers of the early twentieth century still cut evergreens for a lean-to shelter, or slept out under the
stars. Canvas "Duluth Packs," "Whelen Rucksacks," and pack baskets,
the kind still offered by the venerable firm of L.L. Bean, got the hiker
to his destination. Sleeping bags, like the early rucksacks, were made
of canvas or a treated material commonly known as cotton "duck."
No space-age fibers filled these early sleeping bags, but down stuffing
was used extensively then as it is now. The featherbed, after all, was
one of the great institutions of the nineteenth century. The contents
of early backpacks were strikingly similar to the contents found in the
streamlined nylon models used by modern hikers. The *Outdoorsman's
Handbook* recommended a list of essentials that weighed only thirty-
three pounds total (I've carried a lot heavier pack than that), including
Nessmuk's own insect repellent formula of "3 oz. pine tar, 2 oz. castor
oil, and 1 oz. pennyroyal oil, simmered together over a slow fire."

You might be surprised to discover that lightweight freeze-dried
or dehydrated foods are nothing new. The May 1915 issue of *Forest and
Stream* recommended a list of "compressed foods," including an extremely versatile item called "erbwurst." This apparently delicious

compound of various vegetables and meats could be sliced off and eaten raw, boiled in stews and soup, or added to other dishes. Erbwurst was of German origin, and many an American doughboy in World War I delighted in "liberating" a pound or two of the stuff whenever German prisoners were taken. Sporting writers highly recommended that campers purchase fresh eggs and bacon in transit from local farmers. Powdered milk, however, was highly recommended and widely used as a staple in the diets of early sportsmen (as were freshly killed trout).

Today, camping of all varieties is still an important recreation in the West and throughout the nation. Perhaps the old custom of camping out in a wall tent for two or three weeks has been replaced with spending the same period of time in a well-endowed motorhome, but even that practice is nothing new. The first prototype motorhome to enter Yellowstone National Park was a boxlike structure, not unlike modern camper shells, built around the frame of a Model T Ford in 1923. Motorhomes have been a familiar feature in the park ever since that year. In the 1980s, of course, they are more glamorous, just as fly-fishing is supposed to be now.

I once met a guy fly-fishing on the Henry's Fork who had the typical rig of the '80s. It had everything—air conditioning, shower, television set, the works. The walls were plastered with bumper stickers advertising chic ski resorts throughout the West. His refrigerator was well stocked with Corona beer, and he even had a magazine rack containing the latest issue of the *Banana Republic Catalog* conveniently placed within easy reach of the self-contained portapotty. The guy himself was the perfect match for his motorhome. He wore a fuzzy European-style fedora with little pewter and silver nymph and mayfly pins stuck in the crown. His new khaki shirt was well starched, and he smoked a pipe. He was fishing a #10 Royal Trude in the middle of a midge hatch, however, and the fly dragged through the water leaving a V-shaped wake along the sides like a navy PT boat. He did manage to keep his pipe lit in the stout breeze, though. As I'm sure you can tell, although I owned a camping vehicle once myself, I prefer a small tent and a crackling campfire in the deep woods. I even take along an old item of camping gear now and then to remind me of what it might have been like years ago—it's a pleasant tradition. I just make sure to leave the wood axe in the garage at home.

Bear Stories

Every fly-fisher worth his reputation has a good bear story to tell. It's mandatory! If you spend enough time tramping the wilderness in search of new places to fish, sooner or later you will see a bear. I can practically guarantee it. If you make your camp in the western U.S., you may encounter two kinds of bear – *Ursus americanus* and *Ursus arctos*. Let us hope that you meet the former. Take my word for it, grizzly bears are no fun, although a mother black bear with cubs potentially can be just as dangerous. Black bears range in color from light cinnamon through jet black. Grizzlies, sometimes called silvertips because of their shiny coloration at maturity, are much larger and are distinguished by an obvious hump over the shoulders and a more flattened, dishlike face. Black bears are more numerous and roam throughout the mountainous West, while grizzlies fortunately are found only in and around Yellowstone and Glacier national parks and in western Canada and Alaska. The bad news is that some of the best trout fishing in the world is located in grizzly territory.

Take heart; the chance of being injured by a bear is minimal in comparison with other hazards (like driving to work), and your encounter should provide you with a good tale to relate to your friends for years to come. What you make out of the encounter after it's over is the important factor. To put it another way, it's not so much what specifically took place between you and the bruin as how you tell the story afterward. Don't be shy in your storytelling. After all, when you spin your yarn to comrades around a glowing fire at your next camp, you will be engaging in a ritual as old as the nation itself.

From the time of our first Colonial settlements, sportsmen frequently have gathered to relate their hair-raising experiences in the out-of-doors. Stories of hand-to-hand engagements between man and beast are common throughout the nineteenth century. Armed with only a Bowie knife or handy rock (rifles always seemed to be just out of reach), the lone frontiersman always seemed to come out the victor when combating furious bears. Even today, many national outdoor magazines still feature personal columns recounting sportsmen's "near misses" with bears and other wild animals.

In the far West after the Lewis and Clark Expedition in 1806, the legendary fur trappers were the first Americans in significant numbers to meet up with *Ursus arctos*. The code of honor of these mountain men was demanding, and consequently their accounts of doing mortal combat with wild beasts are wrought with much self-acclaim. In fact, the reputations of individual mountain men could be forged by such daring exploits. Around their sun-bronzed necks might hang an aboriginal necklace adorned with their trophies—the fearsome-looking claws of grizzlies, black bears, and other beasts. Like medieval warriors, when two trappers met in the wilderness, the customary greeting included epithets and boasts of great personal deeds. "Who are you?" one trapper would shout across the mountain wilderness as a mysterious rider thundered into view on the back of a spirited pony. Immediately, a boisterous reply would resound through the crisp high-country air: "I'm the man who kilt the bear that skinned Jim Bridger's ass."

Wild animals posed a real threat to the early trappers on a frontier often devoid of nearby settlements or medical services. But as enterprising pioneers pushed the borders of civilization steadily westward after the Civil War, and towns were carved from the hostile land, the habitat of the animals receded toward distant mountain peaks, and life-and-death encounters with bears became less frequent. By the 1880s most of the people seriously confronting bears were sportsmen; hunters, and especially trout-fishers, who frequented the backcountry during the warm months. By this era, the stories told back in town were more jocular in nature, since the sportsman in question usually survived the incident. In fact, these stories today, especially the humorous ones, comprise one of the most common themes to be found in the folklore of the West. Whimsical episodes of this kind have actually come to characterize western literary tradition to a significant degree.

"American humor," states folklorist Mody C. Boatright, "is a key to the American mind." During an age which ostensibly produced this nation's greatest literary achievements along eastern shores, there were scores of westerners tramping through the woods in search of furs or gold (or trout) who every so often were forced to elude hostile Indians, angry bears, and even the occasional mountain lion thrown in for good measure. Miraculously, their exploits have since formed a body of folk literature almost as important to our cultural heritage as the voluminous classics produced by New England's whiskered aesthetics. According to Boatright, the rigors of western living, and the spine-tingling, frequently hilarious tales that emerged from that experience were simply more fascinating to westerners than Emerson's transcendental speculations, or Whitman's glorification of the divine average, or Longfellow's poetic epics. In essence, "it was not that the frontiersmen were universally unlettered. Many of them were emphatically not so. It was that the facts surrounding them, their own experiences, were more intense than anything they could have read." It was humor, which these people used to mock the perils of living in a dangerous land, that shaped much of the western character.

It is not surprising that many of the most waggish bear stories from the past involve trout-fishers. Unlike the ever-observant big game hunter, dependent upon his keen skills as a tracker, fishermen were practically always preoccupied with rod, reel, and the drift of the fly when they became abruptly acquainted with their bears. If freshly killed trout or salmon were dangling from a nearby tree limb, one need not speculate for very long as to why the bruin in question was attracted to the scene. An old Colorado trapper turned prospector by the name of Joe Showers learned that principle the hard way on a fishing trip to the headwaters of the Rio Grande River during the waning years of the nineteenth century.

Joe was perched on a large rock about to take a fly from one of the biggest trout he had landed that day when something suddenly slapped the side of his head with such force that he was knocked into the river below. When Joe rubbed the water from his eyes, he was shocked to see one of the largest bears he had ever encountered. The brute was enjoying an impromptu lunch of big trout, seated on a rock shelf that Joe had occupied just moments before. Having consumed the first fish, the voracious bear grabbed the one that Joe had been taking from the hook when he was so rudely swatted. Joe had been fishing two gaudy wet flies in tandem, using a dropper line knotted a foot or so above the end of his silk-gut leader. The lower, stretcher fly was still in the trout's mouth. When the bear took a bite out of the big fish, its lower jaw suddenly fell open. The beast let out a powerful howl. The hook had somehow imbedded itself in the bear's mouth so that every time the animal attempted to close its jaws, the hook would push further into the sensitive part of its mouth. Finally, the animal shook its head violently and bellowed in pain. At that instant the fly on the dropper swung around and fastened tightly into the animal's left nostril.

"Guess I got you now, you 'tarnal varmint!" Joe shouted as he quickly swam ashore and picked up a big stone. Cautiously, he moved forward. The animal was furious. It stood its ground and turned to meet Joe's assault. When the bear swung around, the fly line caught on a shrub and pulled taut. The bear came up on its hind legs and howled even louder. At that instant Joe hurled his stone, hitting the bear firmly on its nose where the dropper fly was imbedded. The bear tumbled and the leader drew taut and broke, but that same action drove the lower hook a quarter inch deeper into the animal's tongue. The angry bear regained its footing and rushed Joe. The pair clinched, and in the struggle that ensued, man and bear tumbled off the rock shelf together and plunged into the river. Reaching the shallow water, Joe succeeded in finding another stone in the river bottom and began pounding at the bear.

Unknown to them, the duo were being rapidly swept downriver toward a precipitous waterfall. Joe realized the danger too late. In an instant they were over, the miner still clinging to the mad bear. Twenty feet below, the struggle went on until the combatants were dashed against a huge boulder in the swift rapids. This cooled the bear's temper, and it began swimming toward a flat rock on the near shore, the only apparent safety in sight. Joe saw the rock also and succeeded in beating the bear to the perch. Struggling in the fast current, Joe pulled himself onto the rock. The bear was close behind. Slowly Joe got to his feet, and just as the bruin was about to gain the rock, the old prospector let loose a violent kick with his leather boot. The footing was slippery, however, and Joe fell once again into the raging torrent with the bear. There was nothing to prevent man and bear from being carried by the force of the current, and they were swept through a narrow canyon and on to a violent plunge down yet another cataract. This last descent was enough for the bear. It swam for the far bank. Eventually Joe gained high ground himself and collapsed beside the river. After regaining consciousness, the miner followed the river downstream to a nearby Mineral County saloon, where the bartender patched him up and the patrons supplied him with drinks for the next two hours.

In telling his story to the men in the saloon, Joe Showers was animated. "If I'd er done what I otter did," he snorted, "I'd a tuck up that 'thar feeshpole o'mine and played that 'tarnal varmint same as I wud a trout. Then I cud 'a' run him inter my cabin [where his rifle was located] jest as easy as I ever reeled up a fish, but I never a-wunst tho't of it till 'twas too late."

By now you should be getting the idea. I hope your encounter will not be so harrowing as old Joe's, but however harmless it is, you still need to incorporate certain basic factors inherent to telling a good bear story. Joe Showers did. According to B.A. Botkin, one of this country's most eminent folklorists, there are three elements that normally characterize the folklore of the West (especially bear stories). First, there must be an element of violence, or at least the remote potential for violence. Essentially, this criterion assumes that you at least *saw* a wild bear up close. Second, the story must tend to depersonalize man to some degree. This is the most important ingredient. The folklore of the West is based on the pioneer's struggle (usually alone) to conquer the forces of nature or the uncivilized elements of the frontier, i.e., the wilderness, weather, Indians, wild animals, etc., which always assume the role of antagonist in these stories. Usually man, or more accurately, the Anglo-Saxon race, symbolically represented by a single individual, ultimately wins (or at least survives) in these stories only after much effort (that's the great myth of the frontier). Third, the story must have an element of fantasy, "which may be apparent at first glance but is just as likely to be hidden deep down at the roots." The reason for including some degree of fantasy is sheer vanity. After all, the hero presumably had a frightening experience. Fantasy soothes the ego and makes the hero look good despite the fact that he had a basically depersonalizing experience.

The theme of the storyteller as the tragic figure, in essence, is what makes western yarns different from the folklore of other parts of the country. According to Botkin, "In the humor of all other sections one basic situation is the sly country yokel outwitting the city slicker who had taken him for a simpleton. For generations this fable has caressed the self-esteem of rural populations, but it does not often turn up in the West. There are no western yokels." The West, he claims, "is the most cosmopolitan section and probably the most sophisticated." Consequently, western humor tends to be "self-depre-catory." The only exception might be when the white man is pitted against the Indian, but even this theme symbolizes the native Ameri-can as a force of nature, more sophisticated in his relationship with the environment, and although the white man might overcome the Indian in the end, he is still depreciated by the experience and there-fore becomes the butt of the humor.

Now, the basic events of your bear story may grow in the retell-ing, and that's alright so long as you never waver in the premise that what you are saying is nothing except the absolute truth (of course you may want to keep your fingers crossed behind your back while doing so). But the important factor which you must always remem-ber is that the story must be, to some degree, self-deprecatory. In other words, the joke's on you.

The most fascinating thing about bear stories is that they are time-less. They haven't changed much since the frontier years, and conse-quently they allow you a link to the pioneer past. My personal bear story occurred in the pine-clad White Mountains of central Arizona during the spring of 1976. I had just completed grading final exams at the small college where I was teaching, and my partner Dick and I decided to take off a couple of days and go fly-fishing. We were camped in a picturesque little grove of ponderosa pine beside Big Diamond Creek on the Fort Apache Indian Reservation. After break-fast on our first day, we hoisted daypacks and hiked several miles up-stream. Our plan was to fish back down the stream, reaching camp by midafternoon. Ten- to twelve-inch browns and rainbows were breaking water quite actively that day, rising to a fairly consistent hatch of gray midges. Dick and I tied #20 Adams patterns to our twelve-foot leaders. We soon discovered that we could get strikes if we held our rod tips high. In this fashion we would be able to lay out the less-visible leader while keeping the bulky fly line off the wa-ter. Confidently, we crouched down on our knees in the grass, so we would not cast a shadow, and made short casts to the flat pools on the small stream. The tactics worked. We caught and released at least thirty trout that morning.

According to plan, we crested a small sage-covered hill in front of our camp about 2:00 P.M. And there we stopped dead in our tracks. "Why is that tent shaking?" Dick asked. "How should I know?" I replied, while circling around the pine grove to get a look at the tent's entrance. Suddenly, my mouth went dry. I froze. There, with its big rump gloriously protruding from the tunnel entrance of our Sierra Designs three-season tent, was one of the biggest black bears I have ever seen in the wild. It was an old sow, and she was obviously hungry. I tried to recall what I had read about bears, and for a moment, I actually considered climbing the nearest tree – but only for a moment (when was the last time you saw a mature ponderosa pine with climbable branches less than twenty feet off the ground?).

Dick was now standing beside me with his mouth wide open. "Would you just look at that," he said to no one in particular. "I'll bet she's cleaned us out." Feeling rather foolish, now that we realized the food should have been hung in a tree away from the tent, we could do little except stand there and watch the bruin conclude its gastronomic orgy. Pretty soon, though, we actually got brave. "Shoo, you ugly monster," I shouted, while we slowly stepped backwards into the stream, under the somewhat instinctive but nevertheless ridiculous assumption that standing in two feet of water would render us immune to bear attack. "Get out of here and leave us a can of prunes, at least!" (Not that we really needed the prunes' medicinal benefits at that very moment, mind you.) Finally the bear squirmed her way out of the tent. In her mouth was a paperback copy of *Jaws* by Peter Bench-ley. Within seconds the old bear turned around, looked at us, gave a muffled "huff," and unceremoniously lumbered off across a nearby jeep road and climbed up an adjacent mountainside. "Thank God," Dick said, and we began the laborious task of repairing our camp.

For the next half hour or so we didn't say much to one another. We were embarrassed. We had thought of ourselves as outdoor experts – true westerners in the classic sense. Little did we know that the most serious threat to our wounded pride was at that very moment grinding up the jeep road toward our campsite. This threat took the form of a young White Mountain Apache conservation officer driving a four-wheel-drive truck with the official logo of the Fort Apache Reservation embossed on the door. We flagged him down and told him about the marauding bear.

"Damn!" he exclaimed. "That ol' she-bear has been raiding these campsites for the last month. I'm gonna have to tranquilize her and move her up to the Mt. Baldy Primitive Area." I looked at Dick and grinned. "First you have to find her," I said, with an air of confidence in my voice that made me sound knowledgeable in such matters. "No problem," replied the officer. "I'm going to go get my grandfather over at McNary Village. He's a powerful medicine man, and he can recite some chants that will charm that bear right into rifle range." "What!" I said, but the Apache did not reply. "Come on," I laughed, "this is the twentieth century. I'll bet you ten dollars that won't happen." Still the conservation officer said nothing, he just got back in his truck and drove off toward the east. "That's got to be a first in scientific game management strategy," my partner sarcastically replied. "Yeah, that's the last we'll see of him," I smirked, "although it does make me curious. I wonder how much the tribal council pays that guy?"

Much to our surprise, the truck was back within the hour. Actually, we heard it before we saw it. The vehicle's radio was blasting at full volume—"Louie Louie," by the Kingsmen. The truck screeched to a stop near our tent. The young conservation officer jumped down from the driver's seat and ran around to the other side and opened the door. Dick and I sat down on a nearby rock and watched. Slowly, as if partially inhibited by arthritis, a short, wrinkled old man inched his way out of the truck. His hair was snow white, and it flowed down all the way over his shoulders. He wore a bright crimson bandana, rolled up thick and tied around the middle of his high forehead in the Apache tradition of a century ago. He had on a battered pair of leather cowboy boots, a faded pair of Wranglers, and a yellow T-shirt that proclaimed the virtues of Arizona State University. The old man said nothing. He didn't even acknowledge our presence. Instead, he methodically walked several yards out into the middle of the jeep road. He just stood there looking up at the mountain, the gentle slopes of which began on the north side of the road.

After five minutes of staring at the thickly forested mountainside, the old Apache motioned for his grandson to come forward. To our total surprise, the younger man politely asked us to come out on the road and help. We were somewhat shocked. What could we do? We weren't Apache. Wouldn't we be violating some age-old sacred ritual? Besides, what if someone else came along and *saw* us standing there with an Apache medicine man? They might ask, "Whatcha doin'?"

What would our reply be? "Oh gee, we're just chantin' a bear out of the woods." Don't get me wrong; I always relish a chance to learn about different cultures. But, basically I want to do it as an observer— not as a participant. Anyway, I never have, before that day at least, placed much faith in primitive mysticism—especially if I am asked to play a role.

Inevitably, though, our intellectual curiosity got the best of us and we marched out onto the dirt road. In the next minute the four of us were standing there in a line, a history professor, a college administrator, a game warden, and an Apache medicine man wearing an ASU T-shirt, all locking elbows. The old man was on one end of the bizarre line chanting some incomprehensible song in his native Athapaskan tongue. I wondered how long he would make us stay there before giving up. It was almost time for evening fishing, and the White Mountains have excellent diptera hatches around dusk in the nearby lakes. Fat rainbows will literally smash a larvae imitation fished in the surface film; and for once I looked forward to keeping a couple of trout for a camp dinner, since we no longer had any food— not even a can of prunes.

Now, I can't begin to express in words the feeling of horror that came over me when, five minutes later, that old sow bear came charging at full speed down the mountainside as if the woods were on fire. I was trembling horribly when she made her run, but somehow I held my ground. Then, as she gained the road, and I swear this on my sacred, vintage, 1925 model Hardy Perfect fly reel, that bear stopped dead in its tracks and just stared at us with a vague expression on its face. Its eyes appeared to be slightly glazed as if it were in a trance. The medicine man was chanting louder now, obviously reaching some kind of crescendo in his primitive lyric. In the back of my mind I remembered an anecdote about how the old-time Apaches believed the spirits of their ancestors inhabited the souls of wild animals, and I broke out in gooseflesh. Very slowly, and without saying a word, the grandson walked back to the truck, took out his scoped rifle, and loaded the chamber with a big tranquilizer dart. He took careful aim through the scope and expertly squeezed the trigger. There was a muffled report that echoed up the mountainside. The bear twitched her hind leg as the dart struck deeply into her left haunch. She started to trot down the road but stopped almost immediately, listing to one side. A couple of minutes later she dropped down on her belly, almost asleep.

As if nothing unusual had happened, the conservation officer and his grandfather expertly rolled the bear onto a canvas sling, with our help, and then we very gently lifted the animal into the bed of the truck with the assistance of the vehicle's electric winch. Five minutes later the two Apaches were bumping down the jeep road in full four wheel drive with the unconscious bear and my ten bucks. Over the truck radio the Beatles were singing, "I want to hold your ha-a-a-nd." Dick and I went over to nearby Bog Lake to fish for rainbows. We didn't do too well. We missed a lot of strikes—just couldn't concentrate.

I know, you're thinking it was a coincidence. Perhaps the bear had formed the habit of coming down the mountain every day at that time to raid another camp, and the game warden knew it. After all, I did bet the man ten dollars. But, I'll never believe it was coincidental. Not after I saw the hypnotic expression on that bear's face when she so abruptly stopped her charge.

In any event, no one was hurt, and no one had to wrestle with the bear. Today that rarely happens. But the old-timers, we already know, usually had to fight their bears, at least in the stories that made

it into print. You already know about Joe Showers. Another example is the experience of a Wyoming cowboy known to history only as "Bear George." During the fall of 1885, George decided to do some trout fishing up along the Jakey's Fork of the Big Wind River. There were grizzlies in that region in those days, and George found himself in the worst of all possible situations—he startled a mother grizzly with two cubs. The sow almost killed George, but somehow he was able to grab his Winchester from the saddle holster on his frightened horse and shoot the bear.

George took the two cubs home and tamed them. He even learned to ride them, bareback. One of the cubs ran off within a few months, but the remaining pet bear grew up and developed a "fine silver tip after about two years." Eventually, George took the bruin with him on fishing trips into the backcountry for protection from wild grizzlies. The cowboy and his bear would pitch camp right next to a trout stream, and George would build a fire and grease the frying pan. Meanwhile, the bear would get the evening supper. According to George, "the bear'd wade into the stream and look sharp. Sure enough, down would splash that big paw and [the bear would] come out with a trout spinning on one claw. A few twists and a snap, and the cleaned trout was in the pan. Used to toss 'em clear up from the creek," George would boast.

On one trip the bear became quite nervous, however. It started to howl uncontrollably, and George had to hit him on the side of the head with a cast-iron skillet in order to shut him up. He didn't mean to do it, but George caught the bear in the mouth with the heavy skillet and knocked out several of its teeth. George felt bad about having done this, especially when the pet bear suddenly ran from camp and trotted over the nearby hill. George followed, and when he crested the hill he spotted two wild grizzlies rapidly coming across a bend in the river, presumably to snatch the freshly caught fish in his camp. Apparently, George's bear had gone out to defend its master. It met the two wild grizzlies head on. All three bears raised up on their hind legs and were soon tearing at each other's throats. Feeling a bit sorry about the incident with the skillet, George decided to help his bear. He began to run toward the sound of the roaring, fighting grizzlies. One of the wild bears turned and attacked George, and the pet bear came to the rescue, saving George's life. Soon the cowboy was back in the thick of the fight. "I grabs me a piece of tree," he later reported, and "wades in [the river], cracking snoots and thumping skulls, trying to get my bear out of the mess he was in."

George took the worst of it, though, for he was knocked unconscious by the swat of a giant paw. When he woke up, the fight was over. Only his pet grizzly remained on the scene. But something was wrong. The animal was nervous, walking around its master, staring curiously at him. George grabbed the animal and tried to mount its back, but the bear clearly did not wish to be ridden. The cowboy shook at the animal's head and slapped its ears. Finally, George succeeded in mounting the bruin, but when he tried to ride him home, the beast became uncontrollable. The bear crashed off through the woods in the wrong direction, rambling around in tight, meaningless circles, trying to throw off its rider. It took most of the night to get the bear pointed in the right direction down the mountain toward home. Finally the pair reached George's line cabin at daybreak. The bear lay down, exhausted from the fight and the rough trip down the mountainside.

"I never saw such a tired bear," George said. "Not a hair was stirring. And that worried me, seeing as I'd been so cussed that afternoon, throwing the skillet and all." So George got down beside the bear to see if its mouth was still raw from being hit so hard. He pulled open the animal's jaws and looked in. Surprisingly, the mouth was dry but not raw. That wasn't all. To George's utter amazement, the bear had a full set of teeth. Apparently, when the cowboy was unconscious during the fight, the real pet grizzly had taken off, and George had ridden home one of the wild ones.

"Preposterous," you say, "just a typical cowboy yarn told around the cook fire at roundup time." Maybe. But, at least the tale is constructed properly. The three basic elements of a good bear story are present. George probably did have a pet bear he took with him on fishing trips, and he probably was attacked near camp by wild grizzlies, hence the element of violence. He probably was embarrassed that the grizzlies got the best of him in the fight and that he couldn't recognize a wild bear from his pet, hence the element of self-deprecation. As a result, George might have slightly fantasized the actual events by inflating his riding abilities in order to soothe his bruised ego and avoid being chided by his fellow drovers. At least he stuck to his story. George swore up and down that the portrayed events were the "honest truth." Maybe they were. Stop and think about it for a minute. Haven't other people tamed and even ridden grizzlies? In fact, George's encounter is really not all that much more fantastic than my personal tale of an Apache medicine man charming a bear down from the mountains. And I can assure you—that story is completely true.

The Old Fishing Lodge

Old fishing lodges, like fine vintage brandy, are treasured in the memory forever. Their time-worn timbers and thick-paned windows spark the pulse, like the rare discovery of a precious antique. As the imagination takes over, we are compelled to wonder: What has this place seen? There is no stereotype of a classic fishing lodge. For some, a huge, Gothic, latticework hotel in the Adirondacks might fulfill the design, or perhaps an old, weathered Maine "camp" in the lakes region. For others, a white clapboard Victorian inn in the Catskills, over the decades serving as a gathering place for some prestigious fishing club, can evoke treasured memories and a sense of ambiance appropriate for its stature in the world of fly-fishing. In the West, however, these venerable institutions are less common. Perhaps an aging log cabin, built years ago on the forest edge along the shores of some wilderness high lake, fits the image most perfectly. In the end, each fly-fisher must define, according to fond reminiscences, what constitutes a "fishing lodge."

Today, along Montana's Big Hole and other famous western rivers, there are modern lodges and ranches that cater to the elite. One may find freshly picked wildflowers gracing cut-crystal vases on the white table linen at dinner. Gourmet meals are served late, after the evening rise. A classical guitarist might perform the adagio from Rodrigo's *Concierto de Aranjuez* as satisfied fly-fishers uncork a bottle of Chateauneuf du Pape and toast the day's fishing. For many anglers, though, a truly classic western lodge must have a time-tested egalitarian heritage, like the frontier that gave birth to it. Perhaps it is appropriate that my favorite fishing lodge is located in one of the oldest and most frequently visited locations of the angler's West, Yellowstone National Park.

My lodge is not the oldest on record. By 1886 there were three hotels in Yellowstone. All of them employed men to supply their kitchens with freshly caught trout, a tradition widely practiced, though illegal even then. My lodge was built by frontier methods in the Firehole Basin amidst the howling snows of 1903–1904. It was not intended specifically to be a lodge for fishermen, but many have used it for such over the decades. It was built of logs, lodgepole pine, hand-hewn and mortared, and sledded over a winter landscape from several miles away. Its gabled lobby, lofty with gnarled beams and balconies, rhyolite foundation, and massive stone fireplace create for the weary traveler an overwhelming sense of the surrounding wild land. It is called the Old Faithful Inn, and its designer, Robert Reamer, demonstrated remarkable ingenuity in making it sensitive to, and compatible with, the natural environment. It almost seems to be an intrinsic feature of the wilderness landscape.

The Inn was intended to house affluent tourists making the hard trip over muddy forest roads by horse-drawn coach from the Grand Canyon of the Yellowstone. Old Faithful Geyser was, of course, the destination, and prior to the Inn's completion, no first-class hotel stood in the Firehole Valley. During its first years, a man might feel most proper wearing a silk tie, and young ladies in linen dresses would dance with army officers, charged in those years with administering the national park, beside the stone fireplace in the fading evening light. But Old Faithful Inn was located in the "peoples' park," and more modern travelers would have none of its proposed aristocratic image. Today, the visitor of humble means can spend the night in a room next to American dignitaries or nobility from foreign lands. The Inn is fulfilling its role as a metaphor for traditional western ideals.

During the early years of this century, visiting sportsmen could walk a few hundred yards from the massive wood doors of the Inn and catch their twenty-fish limit of big brown trout, which were then taking hold in the Firehole River. After a few days of this sport, the angler could make the trip to the Yellowstone itself and fish for native cutthroats. After a day of casting on the great river, the weary fly-fisher would rest his head on a feather pillow in the old Canyon Hotel. That was the golden age of fishing Yellowstone waters.

Since I was old enough to drive an automobile over long distances,

I have lodged at the Old Faithful Inn while fishing park streams. It is hard for me to realize, sometimes, that the vast majority of lodgers staying there are *not* fishermen. For many, the huge lobby of the Inn is its charm. But for me, it is the guest rooms that best herald the story of its past. In 1913 and again in 1928 the Inn was enlarged with the addition of two wings totaling 250 rooms. But I always stay in the original part of the hotel, even though I must walk down a long public corridor to the newer wing in order to visit the bathroom and take a shower.

I remember an August evening spent in one of those rooms. I turned in before dusk, for I had an appointment in the morning with a McKenzie River driftboat and a West Yellowstone guide employed by Madison River Outfitters. My heart raced with anxiety. I was going to float the Madison River for eight hours, but the weather had been sunny and hot, with the river low and gin clear. The fishing would be maddeningly tough. The bigger rainbows and browns would be skittish, hiding secretively beneath the undercut banks. It would take some skill, perhaps more than I possessed, to entice them out from their secure holes. Stone fly nymphs might be the only way to do it, and I did not look forward to keeping a weighted nymph drifting drag free all day long by holding my rod arm high around my head.

Within a few short minutes, however, the mystique and ambiance of the room soothed my emotion. Beyond my rustic dormer window, draped in lace curtains then as it had been in 1904, I knew that throngs of sightseers would be awaiting the twilight eruption of Old Faithful. The one drawback to the Inn is the myriad of tourists outside the walls. But that sight can easily be overcome, if the mind is willing. Slowly, my imagination drifted off to a simpler age of fewer tourists and more room to cast a fly. I could see the massive front doors of the Inn from my window, and I imagined what it would have been to walk through those portals in an earlier decade. I could visualize a sporty fly-fisher from the early years of the century. He might have ridden the "Yellowstone Special" of the Northern Pacific Railroad up from Ogden, Utah, to the stone depot at West Yellowstone and then made the bumpy ride along the upper Madison by a horse-drawn tallyho coach painted brilliant yellow, or in later years by limousine or touring bus.

The team would pull up beside the entrance. By the late '20s, buses would halt under the new porte-cochere to debark their passengers during an afternoon mountain thundershower. A bellhop would rush out and grab up the angler's leather valises, heavy with fishing tackle. The huge iron hinges on the doors would screech, as the originals still do today, and the angler would march up to the front desk and register while his luggage was taken to his room. After a meal in the dining room, the angler might read a newspaper by the blazing fireplace while rocking in one of the roughhewn chairs. Navajo rugs, hung on the walls in 1904, might arouse his curiosity. Eventually he would retire to his room, perhaps the very room in which I was staying.

I became aware of the well-worn, four-poster iron bed in which I lay, probably original. How many knicker-clad fly-fishers like the one I had imagined had hung their hats on one of those posts? I got up and opened the latticed window. A distinct chill permeated the room as the alpenglow spread over the mountains flanking the Firehole Valley. The steam rising from the geyser basin seemed thicker, ghostlier, and the sweet scent of sage floated into the room on the approaching night air. I noticed the old green dresser. "Old enough to have been here from the beginning," I thought. I wondered how many classic fly reels had sat on that table with loose-coiled silk-gut leaders resting beside them. Perhaps an 1890-model Dame Stoddard & Kendall solid brass reel had graced the table at one time, or maybe a leather Hardy Perfect reel case, rich looking in the mellow light, had once been placed on its surface, under the mirror.

Have you ever considered an old flathead nail? I found one sticking ingloriously out of one of the rough pine logs that comprised the walls of my room. Why was it still there? How many vintage wicker creels had hung from that nail? How many khaki canvas tackle bags, rich with the feel of well-worn leather straps, had been slung unthinkingly over this innocuous object? Bamboo rods, Leonards, Paynes, Garrisons, which would today command a fortune, could have leaned against the wall as incongruously as modern graphites do now, prevented from falling to the plank floor by that simple nail. How many pairs of waders, beat-up wooden landing nets, Wulff vests, and L.L. Bean fishing jackets had come to rest on that little piece of rusting iron?

I suddenly realized that that simple nail, and the room itself, had endured a long span of our fly-fishing heritage in the West. When anglers first stayed here they might have spread out their leather and fleece fly books on that very table in my old room. Inside would be

a gaudy selection of snelled wet flies. Did the browns in the Firehole
River actually rise for those things back in 1904? I remember thinking
that if they were anything like the browns in the Firehole today, they
probably did not, and that's why dry-fly fishing, and eventually
nymphing, became so popular after the importation from Europe of
that challenging species of trout. A canvas case of aluminum tubes

containing my graphite fly rods stood over in one corner where fine split-bamboo once rested. Tomorrow, I would cast weighted nymphs. When the room where I stayed lodged its first fly-fishers, most of them had never even heard the word "nymph," let alone how to tie or fish one. The exact imitation of trichoptera I hoped to employ on the following evening was only a radical new theory when anglers first slept here. And who ever heard of nylon leaders back in 1904? I felt almost overwhelmed when I realized how far my sport had evolved in the past 100 years, how much knowledge and theory I possessed, about which those earlier guests were ignorant.

Finally, I fell asleep under the heavy blankets as the cool mountain air engulfed the ghosts in my room. To this day I have to consult my angling log to recall how successful my fishing was on the Madison River the following day. I can never remember for any length of time, and I am always amazed to rediscover that it was very good. I guess it wasn't that important in the first place. What I do remember with crystal clarity, however, were the features, both tangible and imagined, reflected in the warm glow of that small room in my old fishing lodge. I distinctly can recall drifting off to sleep on that summer evening, realizing once again what I had known for a long time—that there really are many aspects of fly-fishing to ponder and cherish besides catching trout.

Growing Old

If you are anything like me, you dread the day when old age finally halts your activities on the stream. Also, if you are like me, you probably never gave a second thought to that unacceptable reality when you were a kid. I suppose that's what makes being a kid so great—they never consider death as the ultimate reality. The urgent prospect of growing up is the ultimate goal of kids, and for some, fishing is an important part of growing up.

I remember that golden time with fondness; the memories are like yellowing old photographs in a family scrapbook. My friend Denis and I would look forward each summer to fishing Missouri's Roaring River and Bennet Spring Creek. As teenagers we ventured into the Rockies each August to fish for brook trout.

One of the trout streams of our youth was the Fall River. It wasn't much of a river, really. In some spots you could practically jump across it in your hip boots. But it meandered through a pristine mountain meadow, alive in summer with purple daisies, phlox, and Indian paintbrush. In the fall, elk and bighorn sheep would graze in the willows over our shoulders as we tied our flies to the end of our tippets. The river's crystal pools held respectable numbers of nine-inch brook trout, some larger. It was the idyllic stream for a couple of kids. We would drift a big, weighted Hare's Ear nymph in the deep pools and along undercut banks, and the brookies would respond just like they were supposed to. We would yank them unceremoniously up onto the bank and pounce on them in the oily grass with both hands and knees. We might sit there for what seemed like hours, Denis and I, with grass stains on our Levis, just admiring their wildness and their beauty.

These fish of high altitude were hued on the back with a glistening shade of emerald. They had round lateral spots of rich turquoise and bellies of deep crimson. We knew they had been made that way just for us and us alone.

One time while fishing the Fall River, we talked about death. Denis thought he would never die.

"It's all in your mind," he said. "If you don't want to die, you won't."

"But let's pretend we want to," I replied. "If we had to, what would be the neatest possible way to do it?"

After some big-time contemplation (and a few more fish), we concluded that the best way to go would be by cardiac arrest at the age of 103, brought on by the sudden shock of setting the hook into the jaw of a thirty-inch brown trout. Despite the frantic efforts of the beautiful lady stockbroker, who admired us so much she followed us on all our fishing trips (that sort of female behavior was admired when we were sixteen), whoever had caught the trout wouldn't respond to the magnum shots of Chivas Regal repeatedly poured down his throat. The trauma of hooking the big trout would just be too much. She would stand there crying, and with a tight death grip on his fly rod, the lucky fisherman would simply be pulled into the river by the huge fish, and, like the Vikings of old, be gently transported into fisherman's Valhalla.

There have been many fishing trips to the Fall River and many crimson-colored brook trout since that day when I was sixteen. Mostly I took the little stream for granted. Year after year the scenery was always the same. I got to know every pool and riffle. I had the caddis and mayfly hatches pretty well timed. Nothing changed much. The stream always yielded an abundance of brook trout. Occasionally, I even tied into an old hermit brown. But the fishing became predictable, calculated, and expected. I knew it would go on forever; that I might live forever, fishing it every summer. It was like chumming around with a childhood friend who would never move away or become burdened with the responsibilities of being an adult.

Then, on July 15, 1982, the man-made earthen dam holding the waters of a small lake in the high country strained at its seams, buckled, and then broke. It let go a wall of water down a steep-flowing tributary to my river. By the time the flood reached the Fall it had plunged 2400 feet. Flowing at 4000 cubic feet per second and carry-

ing automobile-sized boulders in its wake, the torrent hit the Fall River early in the morning hours. It leveled the protective willows and ponderosa pines along the banks. At the confluence of the two streams a 200-foot alluvial fan spread out toward the little meadow where Denis and I had fished when we were boys. The chocolate-colored water swept through the town below, leaving water marks four feet high on buildings. Four people lost their lives. Finally, the water swept into a downstream reservoir. Authorities feared the reservoir's dam would break. It did not. A potential disaster for downstream communities had been averted. But the Fall River was gone.

Where I had first learned to nymph fish for trout, there was nothing but silt. The undercut banks had been blasted away. Streambed gravel had been carried into the reservoir below. Protective vegetation was nonexistent along once-productive pools. The damage had only begun, really. With the loss of habitat, the few fish that were not swept away to be stranded and die on high ground after the floodwaters receded were doomed. Siltation would destroy the insect populations and hence the delicately balanced ecosystem so necessary for the survival of a self-sustaining trout population. Skeptics predicted the river might run dirty for years to come.

I was devastated by the flood. My fishing log indicates that I had a successful day on the Fall River the very afternoon before the unfortunate event. I felt as if an era had drawn to a close, as if a chapter in my life had ended. To make matters worse, I was later told that a biologist surveying the damage had found a large brown trout stranded and dead above the receding floodwaters. It measured thirty-four inches—the kind of fish that could transport an old man into fisherman's Valhalla. The next morning when I looked into the mirror, for the first time in my life, a real, live adult looked back at me. My youth was finished. In the death of my river, I first grappled with the uneasy feeling that catches up with us all sometime in early mid-life—the subtle realization that we are, indeed, mortal. Once we understand this basic fact of life, we inevitably ask the question: After we grow old—what comes next?

From that day forward I found myself, unconsciously at times, seeking out others who had come face to face with the realization of their own mortality. I felt very strange, to say the least. How many other people out there had come to grips with the aging process because of a simple incident involving a trout stream? Can fishing be such an important part of our being that it can actually serve as a catalyst that moves us from one stage of life into the next? I found no satisfactory answer to these questions among my usual fishing buddies. They had not yet reached the stage of life I sought to understand. Instead, I found my answer in a bygone era, and it involved a sportsman of some repute.

That man was the legendary western illustrator, Charles Marion Russell, a friend of my great uncle. A real cowboy on the Montana plains at the turn of the century, Russell painted what he had known from experience: the life of the cowboy, the American Indian, and the sportsman. "Charley," as he was known to his friends, was one of the few western artists to receive what he called "dead man's prices" for his work while he was still living. Thanks to his wife and business manager, Nancy, whom he affectionately called Mame ("Nancy the bandit" to art collectors), Charley was able eventually to earn a comfortable living from his illustrations. Today his name is practically a cliché in western art circles. Always preferring the life of a hunter and fisher in the untrammeled out-of-doors, Charley shunned big cities as well as the salon artists of New York.

Once when Mame opened a show for Charley in New York, the cowboy artist wrote to a friend in Montana expressing his impressions of the big city: "It's the lonesomest camp on earth," he said. "By God, I'd be tickled to death just to have met a rattlesnake I'd seen before. . . . Our room, way up off the ground, had only one window an' it opened on a dirty brick wall that wasn't more'n two feet away. Air? Wow! It smelled like the dump pile behind old Frank Lampman's chuck wagon. . . . They [the residents] stay in New York an' damn near starve because they like the excitement of the crowd—that's what they call havin' their toes trampled on forty times a day. She's not for me."

In his artistic expression too, Charley reflected his love of nature and the outdoor life. He tolerated abstraction as long as it expressed the true colors of nature and life in the Old West, especially in regard to the culture of the Plains Indian. Anything less was an abomination to him. "Know why painters are impressionistic?" he once quipped. " 'Cause they can't draw an' they know they can't. So they blur their paintin' an hide their bum drawin'. In one gallery I saw a landscape they were raving about. Color! Why, say, if I ever saw colors like that in a landscape I would never take another drink. A man who would paint such a thing and represent it as a copy of nature must be on the ragged edge."

During a tour of England and France in 1914 a friend tried to persuade Charley to go to Rome. "In Rome you would see many of the world's most wonderful paintings," the friend said. "You might even see the Pope." "I wouldn't go to Rome to see Christ himself," Charley replied. "No sir! I'm goin' back to Montana an' stay there as long as I live." Charley did return to Montana in 1914. He had exactly twelve years to live. Here was a man whose love of nature and the great western wilderness closely paralleled my own views on the subject.

During his last years Charley spent much of his time with his close friend, writer and U.S. Senator-to-be Frank Bird Linderman. In 1917 Linderman constructed a log home on a sheltered cove along Flathead Lake's Goose Bay at the edge of the rugged northern Montana wilderness. Charley would bring his family to stay with the Lindermans while he and Frank would head out on extended hunting and fishing trips complete with a train of pack horses and huge canvas wall tents. "Ho! Ho! Hi-eeeeeee," Charley would shout to his friend in greeting as he approached the Linderman residence. Frank would break into a wide grin of anticipation.

One of their last trips together was into the wilds of the South Fork of the Judith River, which Charley had come to know well as a young cowboy. From reading Linderman's recollections, one can almost sense the feelings Charley was having on these later trips. He knew there would not be many more. Like me, Charley had come to grips with his mortality from his experiences in the out-of-doors. "Say, Frank," Charley said with a very serious expression, "you've always picked our trips. Lemme pick this one, hey? South Fork of the Judith. An' we'll go in from Neihart. I ain't been on the South Fork of the Judith since I was a kid." Charley's expression now seemed urgent. As a youth Charley had hunted and fished the Judith. He remembered the colorful little trout plucked from the riffles of the wilderness stream in his younger years. But a number of years before, the South Fork had experienced a terrible flood, and Charley could not find it in himself to return. Now he wished to see this river of his youth once more before time caught up with him.

The two old friends started out in the fall when the aspen trees were a fiery gold. One evening while encamped in a rustic old wilderness hunting lodge built years ago among the pines along the river, Frank Linderman went out to shoot a deer for supper. Charley, alone now with his thoughts, strung up his rod and went fishing. He had been preoccupied for the previous day or so. Apparently he wanted to catch some of those bright-colored little trout of his youth, perhaps pounce on them with both hands and knees and then just sit there for a while and admire their beauty.

After darkness had fallen over the valley, Frank Linderman came riding back to camp. He dropped a big buck deer off the back of his horse onto the half-frozen ground and entered the lodge. Charley was singing almost mystically, "singin' Injin" songs, Frank mused, in a "high pitched voice so perfectly imitating a red man's that if I had not known him to be alone in the lodge I might have been deceived." When Charley sang "Injin," it was always an important occasion. Charley was singing by the firelight and beating on the bottom of an old beat-up camp kettle with a stick wrapped in a dishrag to make the kettle sound like a tom-tom. Eight brook trout with turquoise spots along the sides and bright crimson bellies were laid out before him on a "finically folded" saddle blanket.

"Singing to them, Russ?" Frank asked, casually.

"Uh-huh," Charley replied without embarrassment. "I wish you coulda seen 'em when I yanked 'em out of the water. They was sure awful pretty before their colors faded!"

That was Charley's way of dealing with the advancing years, of renewing, one more time, the cherished experiences of youth.

The story of Charley Russell and the brook trout has come to mind often since my Fall River flooded. Here was a man I truly admired for his human qualities who passed on long before my time. He enjoyed the same pleasures, the same emotions, the same concern about growing old, the same need to relive a simple pleasure of youth. He knew what was truly important in life, and he could put it all into meaningful perspective despite his growing fame and success.

So about a year ago, just like Charley Russell, I returned to the special place of my youth, the Fall River, for the first time since the flood. I took a sixteen-year-old with me. We both caught brook trout. There weren't as many in the pools as there had been before, but they still had bright spots and crimson bellies. We admired them. Caddis flies fluttered above us. There was still some silt built up along the bends in the stream, but the bottom was stabilizing. The trout were returning in what seemed like a long, almost imperceptible, but certain ritual of renewal. Since that day I have never again taken small streams and brook trout for granted. Like people, trout streams may end one day. But somehow I know, just like Charley Russell discovered, there is renewal for both people and trout streams. And as far as I'm concerned, that renewal is "what comes next."

Someday the Fall River may even grow another big brown trout, the kind of fish that could transport an old man to fisherman's Val-

halla. It will take time. Perhaps when that time comes, I will be able to foresee an end to my days on the stream. I have not taken many truly large brown trout on the surface of a small meadow stream, but if that old brown is there I can assure you I will fish for it with a dry fly. It seems only fitting. This time I will be certain to have a flask of Chivas Regal in my fishing vest. I will tie on a stiffly hackled selection and make a gentle cast to the grassy bank on the far side of the deep river bend where the big trout is hiding. The fly will alight no more than a couple of inches from the bank, preferably hitting the grassy bank and then gently dropping into the run. The barbules of my dry fly will gracefully dimple the surface waters of the crystal pool and then drift naturally downstream in the slow, steady current, just like when I was a boy. Perhaps the big brown will rise. If so, I will make sure to have my fly tied to an extra-strong tippet—just in case.

Epilogue:
The Legacy of History

They want to build a dam on the South Platte River. Not just any dam, mind you, but a big one that will wipe out thirteen miles of Gold Medal trout water along Colorado's Front Range. The fight, which might already be lost by the time you have read this book, promises to be one of the most colossal environmental battles in history. Critics claim the new dam will destroy wildlife habitat (in addition to the stream environment) as far downriver as western Nebraska. But, quite simply, the city of Denver needs more water. That's nothing new. Almost every place in the West has *always* needed more water. The question of water rights has provoked bloody feuds since the 1860s. Water, the very essence of life in the West, has never been taken for granted. It has continuously, irrevocably, shaped our history—and it always will.

When I was a boy, my Uncle Bill took me on a fishing vacation to the South Platte River. I matched a hatch of mayflies for the first time in my life. The whole concept of hatch matching had been relatively meaningless to me before that time, although I had been told of it. I caught my first-ever selective brown trout on that trip, a twelve-incher, and I have never forgotten the experience. My Uncle Bill liked to preach a lot about morality. In fact, that characteristic cost him one marriage, and eventually, perhaps, his health as well. But I am of the opinion that stream ethics and environmental concerns should be preached occasionally. Uncle Bill would have been proud of his success with me, I suppose, and I shall never forget what he told me on the trip home.

He said: "For those people who love to fish, there is no more exciting sight in nature than a brown trout rising to a dry fly, and teaching a youngster to catch a brown trout is the finest thing I know." Of course, Uncle Bill's ideals may be practiced on many streams besides the South Platte – at least until some growing city needs even more water. But the fact remains that those thirteen miles of the South Platte are regarded by many as being simply the best trophy trout stream within one hour of a major metropolitan area in the entire U.S.

As we have seen, there were once many quality trout streams in the West, alive with native fish. But in the quest for survival and progress, the cutthroats in these waters were blasted with dynamite to feed expanding human populations, major watersheds were polluted with mining wastes to foster the new economy, and finally, rivers were dammed into oblivion to provide water for agriculture and human consumption. These practices created jobs and increased the standard of living for many, and by a different standard of measurement, that was good. Here were practices that allegedly comprised "the real world." But did the pioneers, eager with dreams and optimism, go too far too fast? Almost assuredly they felt the untapped resources around them would last longer than they did. We cannot really condemn them for their ignorance. Man came to the western frontier and exploited its natural resources mercilessly, but unknowingly, and then suddenly realized that perhaps he had made a big mistake. He simply woke up one morning to discover his gold and silver mines played out, useless scars on the earth, grazing lands eroded, forests decimated, the great herds of free-roaming bison vanished from the face of the earth, and native cutthroat streams barren.

So he tried to make it right again. Mines, a few at least, were filled in, grazing land was restored where possible, remaining forests were preserved and managed selectively, and exotic species of trout were planted in depleted waters. In some cases, man actually improved upon the original state of things, and this is true of trout resources especially, if only on a reduced scale. But history is cyclical. We certainly have improved the quality of fishing today from what it was at the lowest point of human decimation. Still, with some notable exceptions in the case of stocking naturally barren waters and the establishment of foresighted scientific management practices on localized waters, it is not quite at the level it was originally, especially in light of increased angling pressure and continued habitat destruction. To be sure, there are many rivers where an angler can still catch large

brown trout. But can we really afford to lose *any* more world class
trout streams? The South Platte is but one example.

The fact remains, however, that in some cases, man actually *has*
made it right again. The entire history of the West has been determined by the principles of adaptation, innovation, and invention. If
the frontiersman could not at first adapt to the wilderness, he did not
survive at all. If he could not then find new ways to harness the wilderness, he did not survive for very long. Many pioneers found new
ways that exploited nature, and their communities now mostly lie as
rotting ghost towns, blasted by the reclaiming winds. Others, however, replaced what they took from nature and thus have survived in
harmony with their surroundings. But all newcomers had to make
changes and seek alternatives from the patterns of life they had known
before they became pioneers. Seeking new alternatives has always
characterized the lives of westerners who have survived and improved
their quality of life. Water and the other elements of the natural surroundings have always been important variables in the unending quest
for alternatives.

Are there now no alternatives to destroying trophy trout rivers?
Since before this century man has pumped water from one side of
the continental divide to the other, channeled it from somewhere else,
or at least dammed up less recreationally important waters, if any were
available, for commercial use. The costs of these alternatives might
be high, but cannot cost be measured in terms other than money?
Many feel new alternatives could still exist if we only look for them.
During no other period in our history has the fly-fisher had more
opportunity to "make it right again." Since the 1960s national non-
profit organizations like The Federation of Fly Fishers and Trout
Unlimited, and their local chapters, have successfully lobbied and
actively worked to save and improve trout habitat throughout the
nation. Apparently, more and more fly-fishers find the cause important. The membership of TU alone has risen nationally from 17,479
members in 1981 to over 48,000 members by 1987. These organizations
and others, as well as a host of concerned angling writers and just plain
fly-fishermen have long advocated the cause of conservation. Doing
what we can to prevent stream pollution each time we go fishing,
volunteering with some legitimate organization to actively improve
fish habitat, expressing our ideas and opinions in the political arena,
and personally limiting the kill as an essential philosophical ethic of

the sport—these are *individual* responsibilities. In the end, the crusade for creating and maintaining quality fishing is a highly personal endeavor requiring more from us than mere advocacy.

It was, after all, the individualist who tried to win the West. In some cases he succeeded and in some cases he failed miserably. But in all cases he found he had to make changes and seek alternatives if his hopes and dreams were to survive and flourish, even temporarily—such is the legacy of history. Some scholars assert that a society without a history is a society devoid of culture. As we have seen, fly-fishing society has a rich experience with both, perhaps more than any other sport. Can we learn not only the lessons of nature and science, but the lessons of history as well, and thus keep the *productive* human cycles headed in the right directions? Can we continue to seek new and effective alternatives to what we require from nature and man to maintain the aesthetics of the sport? Can we bequeath to future generations, through active individual initiative, the quality of fishing known to our ancestors and to ourselves? Will we still be able, someday, to take our sons and daughters to trophy waters where they can cast a fly, and where we can explain what truly constitutes "the real world," and then be able to say to them with anticipation rather than regret, that teaching a youngster to catch a brown trout is the finest thing we know? I, for one, sincerely hope we can.

Bibliography

This bibliography is basically limited to books and periodicals used as resource material for the subjects examined in the book. Throughout the text I have cited numerous news items from local western newspapers. These articles portray the flavor and attitudes of the respective decades and generations during which they were written and are, thus, an important source of our angling history. Unfortunately, they are so numerous that space does not permit repeating the citations in the bibliography. Where appropriate I have cited specific newspaper items in the text of the book. In addition, book and periodical sources are cited in the text where feasible but are listed in the bibliography as well.

For the reader wishing to learn more about our angling heritage, not only in the West, but throughout the U.S., I suggest *The American Fly Fisher*, the journal of The American Museum of Fly Fishing, and *The Flyfisher*, which is the journal of the Federation of Fly Fishers. Paul Schullery's *American Fly Fishing: A History*, (N.Y.: Nick Lyons Books, 1987) is an excellent book detailing the development of the techniques, ethics, literature, and tools of the sport in the U.S. while John Reiger's *American Sportsmen and the Origins of Conservation*, (N.Y.: Winchester Press, 1975) deals with the history of sportsmen's activities in the conservation movement throughout the nation. They are good places to start learning more about our fly-fishing heritage.

Books

A Pictoral History of Estes Park, Colorado, Estes Park: privately published, 1968.

Bergman, Ray. *Trout*. N.Y.: Alfred A. Knopf, 1938.

Bird, Horace A. *History of A Line*. N.Y.: Press of America Bank Note Company, 1889.

Bird, Isabella. *A Lady's Life in the Rocky Mountains*. Norman: University of Oklahoma Press, 1960. First published 1876.

Boatright, Mody C. *Folk Laughter on the American Frontier*. N.Y.: Collier Books, 1961.

Botkin, B.A., ed. *A Treasury of Western Folklore*. N.Y.: Crown Publishers, 1951.

Brooks, Charles E. *Fishing Yellowstone Waters*. Piscataway, N.J.: Winchester Press/Nick Lyons Books, 1984.

———. *The Living River*. N.Y.: Nick Lyons Books/Doubleday, 1979.

Buchholtz, C.W. *Rocky Mountain National Park: A History*. Boulder: Colorado Associated University Press, 1983.

Burns, Henry. *Angling Books of the Americas*. Atlanta: Angler's Press, 1975.

Chittenden, Hiram Martin. *The Yellowstone National Park*. Norman: University of Oklahoma Press, 1964. First published 1895.

France, Lewis B. *With Rod and Line in Colorado Waters*. Denver: Chain, Hardy & Company, 1884.

Gillmore, Parker. *Gun, Rod and Saddle: Personal Experiences*. N.Y.: W.A. Townsend & Adams, 1869.

Gingrich, Arnold. *The Fishing in Print: A Guided Tour Through Five Centuries of Angling Literature*. N.Y.: Winchester Press, 1974.

Grey, Hugh, and Ross McCluskey, eds. *Field & Stream Treasury*. N.Y.: Henry Holt and Company, 1955.

Hackle, Sparse Grey. *Fishless Days, Angling Nights*. N.Y.: Crown Publishers, 1971.

Haines, Aubrey. *The Yellowstone Story*, vols. 1 & 2. Boulder: Colorado Associated University Press and Yellowstone Library and Museum Association, 1977.

Haig-Brown, Roderick. *The Western Angler*. N.Y.: Morrow, 1939.

Halford, F.M. *Dry Fly Fishing*. London: Barry Shurlock, Publisher, 1973. First published 1889.

Hamilton, Edward, M.D. *Recollections of Fly Fishing*. N.Y.: O. Judd Company, 1885.

Haywood, Jim. *Antiques of Colorado Angling*. Denver: Denver *Post* and Wright & McGill Co., undated.

Henkin, Harmon. *Fly Tackle: A Guide to the Tools of the Trade.* Philadelphia & N.Y.: J.P. Lippincott Company, 1976.

Jennings, Preston. *A Book of Trout Flies.* N.Y.: Derrydale Press, 1935.

Keane, Martin J. *Classic Rods and Rodmakers.* N.Y.: Winchester Press, 1976.

Kelley, Tim. *Tim Kelley's Fishing Guide: The Official Colorado & Wyoming Guidebook.* Denver: Hart Publications, 1983.

Leonard, J. Edison. *Flies.* N.Y.: A.S. Barnes, 1950.

Linderman, Frank Bird, ed. by H.G. Merriam. *Recollections of Charley Russell.* Norman: University of Oklahoma Press, 1963.

Marbury, Mary Orvis. *Favorite Flies and their Histories.* N.Y.: Houghton Mifflin, 1892.

Marinaro, Vincent. *A Modern Dry Fly Code.* N.Y.: Putnam & Sons, 1950.

Mayer, Alfred M. *Sport with Gun and Rod in American Woods & Waters.* N.Y.: The Century Company, 1883.

Melner, Samuel, and Hermann Kessler, eds., with commentary by Sparse Grey Hackle. *Great Fishing Tackle Catalogs of the Golden Age.* N.Y.: Crown Publishers, 1972.

Merrit, John I. *Baronets and Buffalo: The British Sportsmen in the American West 1832–1881.* Missoula: Mountain Press, 1985.

Mitchell, Finis. *Wind River Trails.* Salt Lake City: Wasatch Publishers, 1975.

McClane, A.J. *McClane's Standard Fishing Encyclopedia and International Fishing Guide.* N.Y.: Holt, Rinehart & Winston, 1965.

McDonald, John. *The Origins of Angling.* N.Y.: Doubleday, 1963.

———. *Quill Gordon.* N.Y.: Alfred A. Knopf, 1972.

———, ed. *The Complete Fly Fisherman: The Notes and Letters of Theodore Gordon.* N.Y.: Scribners & Sons, 1947.

Neasham, V. Aubrey. *Wild Legacy.* Berkeley: Howell North Books, 1973.

The Outdoorsman's Handbook. N.Y.: Field & Stream Publications, undated–circa 1920s.

Orvis, Charles F. and A. Nelson Cheney. *Fishing with the Fly.* Boston: Houghton Mifflin Company, 1886.

Reiger, John F. *American Sportsmen and the Origins of Conservation.* N.Y.: Winchester Press, 1975.

Schlissel, Lillian. *Women's Diaries of the Westward Journey.* N.Y.: Schocken Books, 1985.

Schullery, Paul. *American Fly Fishing: A History.* N.Y.: Nick Lyons Books, 1987.

Schweibert, Ernest. *Remembrances of Rivers Past.* N.Y.: MacMillan, 1973.

———. *Trout.* N.Y.: Dutton, 1978.

Scofield, Susan, and Robert Schmidt. *The Inn at Old Faithful.* Bozeman: Crowsnest Associates, 1979.

Shields, George O. *Hunting in the Great West.* Chicago: Rand McNally, 1888.

———. *Cruising in the Cascades.* Chicago: Rand McNally, 1889.

Strong, General W.E. *A Trip to the Yellowstone National Park in July, August, and September, 1875.* Norman: University of Oklahoma Press, 1968. Original journal first published privately circa 1876.

Thomas, D.H. *The Southwestern Indian Detours.* Phoenix: Hunter Publishing Company, 1978.

Trotter, Patrick C. *Cutthroat: Native Trout of the West.* Boulder: Colorado Associated University Press, 1987.

Varley, John D. and Paul Schullery. *Freshwater Wilderness: Yellowstone Fishes & Their World.* Yellowstone National Park: Yellowstone Library and Museum Association, 1983.

Wetzel, Charles McKinley. *American Fishing Books.* Newark: privately published, 1950.

Whitney, James Parker. *Reminiscences of a Sportsman.* N.Y.: Forest & Stream, 1906.

Periodicals

Bates, Joseph D. Jr. "Carrie Stevens and the Gray Ghost." *The Flyfisher* 6, no. 4 (1973): 3–7.

Bilby, Keith L. "Colorado's Threatened Greenback." *Flyfishing the West* 2, no. 5 (1979): 26–29.

Brooks, Charles E. "Return of a River." *Trout* 17, no. 2 (1976): 21 & 33.

Brown, Mark H. "Yellowstone Tourists and the Nez Perce." *Montana* 16, no. 9 (1966): 30–43.

Cameron, Kenneth M. "The Girls of Summer, Part 1." *The Flyfisher* 10, no. 3 (1977): 8–11.

———. "The Girls of Summer, Part 2." *The Flyfisher* 10, no. 4 (1977): 15–17.

————. "Sara McBride: Pioneering Angling Entomologist." *The American Fly Fisher* 5, no. 2 (1978): 10–11.

————. "The Victorian Angler." *The American Fly Fisher* 7, no. 1 (1980): 2–7.

————. "Fly Styles." *The American Fly Fisher* 8, no. 1 (1981): 2–7.

Carnifex, John. "Fishing Along the Pecos." *Outing* (July 1891): 1–8.

Clifton, Charles S. "Recovery Plan Helps Colorado Cutthroats." *Colorado Outdoor Journal* 2, no. 2 (1987): 37–40.

Cockhill, Brian. "The Quest of Warren Gillette." *Montana* 22, no. 3 (1972): 12–30.

"Colorful Greenback Cutthroats Discovered." *Colorado Outdoors* 16, no. 1 (1967): 24.

Cullimore, Clarence. "Along Golden Trout Creek." *Forest and Stream* (June 1917): 198–203.

Cutter, Ralph. "Hooking Mortality Figures." *Fly Fisherman* 18, no. 6 (1987): 12.

Denver Post. Various news clips (1926–1949).

Denver Times. Various news clips (1898–1922).

Denver Field & Farm. Clips (August 10, 1912 and December 1, 1888).

Eggert, Richard. "The Golden Heritage." *Fly Fisherman* 5, no. 3 (1974): 50–62.

Forest and Stream. Various news clips. January 1876, October 1911, December 1911, June 1912, April 1915, June 1917, June 1918, August 1918.

Fort Collins Express. November 23, 1876.

France, Lewis B. "Memories of an Angler." *Western World* (September 1907): 20.

Georgetown Colorado Miner. Clips (August 31, 1887): 3.

Gordon, Theodore. "Opening Day in ye Olden Time." *Forest and Stream* (June 15, 1912): 4.

Grey, Zane. "Colorado Trails." *Outdoor Life* 51, no. 3–6 serialized (1918): 165–398.

Haggerty, Bill. "A Trapper's Lake Tradition." *Colorado Outdoors* (September-October, 1987): 18–21.

Hogan, Austin. "Preserving Our Heritage." *The Flyfisher* 8, no. 3 (1975): 33–35.

Josephy, Alvin M. Jr. "Here in Nevada A Terrible Crime." *American Heritage* 21, no. 4 (1970): 93–100.

Kelley, J.W. "With Rod and Line in the Rockies." *Western World* (August 1907): 19–20.

Langhorst, Minnie Louise. "Traversing the Golden Trout Country." *Forest and Stream* (January 1918): 11–15.

Laybourn, Margaret. "In the Mountains with Finis Mitchell." *Wyoming Wildlife* 41, no. 1 (1977): 26–30.

Lincoln, Robert Page. "Camps, Camping and Cooking." *Forest and Stream* (May 1915): 276.

Logan, Bill. "Bill Phillipson Finds it Easy." *Rocky Mountain News* (September 11, 1975): 93–95.

Lynde, John. "When Flies were Sixty Cents per Dozen." *The Flyfisher* 11, no. 1 (1978): 12.

O'Brien, John R. "The Roads of Yellowstone 1870–1915." *Montana* 17, no. 3 (1967): 30–39.

Orrelle, John. "Evolution of the Fishing Reel." *The Flyfisher* 9, no. 1 (1976): 12–17.

———. "Two Early American Fly Reels." *The Flyfisher* 9, no. 2 (1976): 24–26.

Oswald, Tony. "Colorado's Rarest Trout." *Colorado Outdoors* 36, no. 1 (1987): 8–9.

"Pyramid Lake." *Nevada Highways* 17, no. 2 (1967): 2.

Rathborne, R.W. Jr. "Trout Fishing on the Big Laramie." *Forest and Stream* (June 1, 1912): 284.

Reeves, Thomas C. "President Arthur in Yellowstone National Park." *Montana* 19, no. 3 (1969): 18–29.

Rocky Mountain News. Various clips (1861–1887).

Rountree, Les. "Camping in 1907." *Colorado Outdoors* 23, no. 1 (1974): 36–39.

Schullery, Paul. "The Royal Coachman." *Field & Stream* (January, 1984): 48 & 91–92.

Shafroth, John F. "Fishing in Colorado." *Forest and Stream* (June 20, 1912): 301–304.

Smith, Bob. "Alvord Cutthroat." *Flyfishing* 10, no. 6 (1987): 16.

Stegner, Wallace. "Who are the Westerners?" *American Heritage* 38, no. 8 (1987): 35–41.

Strickland, E.J. "The Federation's First Decade." *The Flyfisher* 8, no. 3 (1975): 36–39.

"Tight Lines" (letter from David A. Cannameia). *Fly Fisherman* 18, no. 3 (1987): 6.

"What Happened to our Fish?" *Wyoming Wildlife* 16, no. 3 (1952): 4–13.

Woodward, Harry R. "A Look Back: A 75-Year History of the Colorado Game, Fish, and Parks Division." *Colorado Outdoors* 21, no. 3 (1972): 1–2.

Unpublished Material

Interview with Helen Blumenschein of Taos, New Mexico, December 21, 1987.

Letters of Maj. Daniel Vanderslice: in possession of the author.

Wolcott, Jewell, interviewer. Oral History of Leroy Holubar. Boulder: Boulder Public Library Oral History Program, January 15, 1986: audio tape.

About the Author

John H. Monnett combines twenty years as a historian of the American West with twenty-five years of experience as an avid fly-fisher. He is a member of the Boulder Flycasters, Trout Unlimited, and The Federation of Fly Fishers. Between fishing trips Dr. Monnett has taught at colleges in Arizona, Missouri, and Colorado. Currently, he teaches western history at Metropolitan State College, Denver, and has authored numerous articles on western history and the outdoors. He is co-author of *Colorado Profiles: Men and Women Who Shaped the Centennial State* (1987), and author of the highly acclaimed regional best seller, *A Rocky Mountain Christmas: Yuletide Stories of the West* (1987).

Index